Genuine Articles

Authentic reading texts for
intermediate students of
American English

Student's Book

Catherine Walter

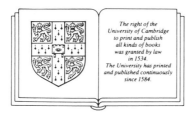

The right of the
University of Cambridge
to print and publish
all kinds of books
was granted by law
in 1534.
The University has printed
and published continuously
since 1584.

Cambridge University Press
Cambridge
New York   Port Chester
Melbourne   Sydney

For Sister Mary Elizabeth McCullough, in gratitude

Published by the Press Syndicate of the University of Cambridge
The Pitt Building, Trumpington Street, Cambridge CB2 1RP
40 West 20th Street, New York, NY 10011-4211, USA
10 Stamford Road, Oakleigh, Victoria 3166, Australia

First published 1986
Fifth printing 1991

Printed in the United States of America

Library of Congress Cataloguing in Publication Data
Walter, Catherine, 1946–
Genuine articles.
1. English language – Text-book for foreign
speakers.   2. Readers – United States.   3. English
language – Study and teaching – Foreign speakers.
I. Title.
PE 1128.W343   1986   428.6′4   85–10993

ISBN 0-521-27800-7 student's book : paperback
ISBN 0-521-27801-5 teacher's manual : paperback

Contents

Part 1 Instructions: How to do things

Part 2 Descriptions: What things are like

Part 3   Processes: How things happen

Part 4   Narrative: What happened

Part 5   Persuasion: Why you should do it

Part 6   Categories: How things are classified

Acknowledgments

I should like to thank Felicia Coates, Charles Dillingham, Christine Tierney, and Elliott Glazer for their helpful suggestions. Special thanks to Michael Swan for his many useful comments, and my gratitude to the Walter family, especially Helen, B.J., and Carolyn, for their generous support. A hug to little Mark for those he did without while I was working on this book.

To the student

Careful studies have been done on people reading texts in their own language where the subject matter was difficult and some of the vocabulary was new. The people who did well under these circumstances almost all dealt with the difficult text in the same way:

1. First they read the text once, carefully, with pauses to think about what they had read.
2. Then they read the text at least once more, pausing from time to time to look at other parts of the text. This was in order to see the connections between different parts of the text, and to build a summary in their minds.

A very large percentage of people who read in this way remember both general ideas and details better than people who read in other ways.

Of course, if you are not used to reading English in this way, deciding to change is not enough. So each text in *Genuine Articles* has a *Summary skills* or similar exercise first. This exercise does not ask you to *write* a summary, but it requires you to look back at the text and organize the information in it. By the time you have finished the book, you will have had enough practice to do this yourself with any text you read.

In addition to summary building, there are other reading skills that are particularly important when you read a foreign language. Certain skills will be necessary for every text you read in English, for example, guessing unknown words.

Others, like realizing what words like *it* mean, will be needed only for certain types of texts. In this book, you will practice these skills with specially designed exercises. Each set of exercises is based on the particular problems of the text it follows, and each exercise aims to help you with one particular skill.

All of the texts in the book are real samples of written English. You will find newspaper articles, advertisements, passages from books of fiction and nonfiction, part of a travel brochure, letters, and poetry. None of them was written especially for foreigners. This means that some texts may be easier to understand than others; but even the easier texts will help you read better. The exercises accompanying difficult texts will give you ways of dealing with other texts outside the classroom. Remember that you can get a lot of information from a text without understanding every word.

There are definitions for a few words in some texts. These words are important to an understanding of the text, and are difficult or impossible to guess. Some difficult words are not defined, but these are not important to an understanding of the text: Do not worry about them. Remember, too, that the definitions given are for the words as they are used in the text; you may want to check with your teacher or look in a good dictionary before using the same word in another situation.

To the student

There are no multiple-choice questions in *Genuine Articles*. There are several reasons for this. One is that while people who have good summary skills do well on multiple-choice tests, the reverse is not always true. So if you are preparing for an examination that includes this type of question, *Genuine Articles* will help you.

This book was written for use in the classroom. However, if you want to use it on your own, there is an answer key to the exercises in the Teacher's Manual.

To the teacher

Genuine Articles aims to equip intermediate students with a range of specific reading strategies, so that they will be able to deal with the variety of written material they meet outside the classroom. Twenty-four authentic texts are accompanied by a series of exercises; each exercise works on one of the skills that make for success in reading difficult texts.

The texts

The range of written material people encounter in their lives is very wide. In order to develop in students the flexibility necessary for dealing with this range of material, four selection criteria were used: authenticity, variety of discourse type, range of subject matter, and diversity of source. Authenticity here means using largely unadapted excerpts of texts not specifically written for non-native speakers. Where some of the texts have been slightly adapted, the changes are of the sort a native speaker would expect in an abridged article or novel: They were made to preserve the flow of the shortened text rather than to simplify the language.

The choice of authentic texts within the book is based on six important discourse functions (instructions, description, process, narrative, persuasion, and categorization). For each function, four texts were selected, each exemplifying the function in a different way. So in Part 4 on narrative, for example, there are texts about a diamond cutter (from a novel), an unusual thief (from a news magazine), mishaps during opera performances (from a book), and chemical contamination (from a newspaper article). Covering all or most of the units as students progress through an intermediate course will thus help prepare them for the many different kinds of texts they may come up against outside the classroom.

However, it is not strictly necessary to follow the order of the units in the book. Because the texts are authentic, length and difficulty vary slightly from one text to the next; there is not a progression in difficulty from the beginning of the book to the end. In addition, the unit based on each text is self-contained, so teachers can feel free to "dip in" to the book, choosing texts that fit into the topics or functions they are dealing with in class. Of course, teachers following a functional syllabus will probably want to use the four units of each part in succession, in order to demonstrate different realizations of the same function.

A note on glosses: A word is glossed only (1) if its meaning is vital to the comprehension of the text and (2) if it cannot be guessed from context. It may be a good idea to point out to your students that the glosses are not dictionary definitions: A gloss covers only the way the word is used in the text.

The exercises

There are a certain number of skills that can be easily assimilated and that provide powerful tools for the foreign-language learner approaching a difficult text. Among these, for example, are skill in guessing words from context and the ability to link a language item (such as *her* or *these areas*) to an earlier element in the text. Each text in *Genuine Articles* is followed by a set of exercises focusing on the particular difficulties contained in it; each exercise concentrates on a single skill. This one-exercise, one-skill approach is designed to give students a clear picture of what they are learning in each unit – something that is not always easy to achieve at an intermediate level and that aids student motivation.

The most important exercise in each unit (usually entitled *Summary skills*) almost always faces the text, and for a precise reason: Its aim is to make students practice the same eye movements that successful native readers use when trying to understand a text whose content and vocabulary are difficult for them. For a detailed discussion of the rationale behind this approach, see the Introduction to the Teacher's Manual and Answer Key.

The Teacher's Manual and Answer Key

The Teacher's Manual gives suggestions for the classroom exploitation of all the exercises, as well as a key to the answers. Because many teachers like to use texts as springboards for other classroom and homework activities, detailed suggestions for follow-up work are also given in each unit, including:

1. Complete instructions for a classroom activity practicing speaking skills and approaching the theme of the text from a different standpoint. This might be, for example, a task-based discussion, a role-play activity, or a class survey.
2. Suggestions for more intensive vocabulary work, designed to help students incorporate some of the words from the text into their active usage.
3. An idea for a writing practice exercise based on the theme of the unit.

Genuine Articles
Student's Book

1   How to shine at a job interview

This is the first page of a magazine article. Read it carefully, as many times as you want. Then answer the questions.

The smart job-seeker needs to get rid of several standard myths about interviewing before starting to pound the pavement looking for a job. What follows is a list of some of these untruths and some tips to help you do your best at your next interview.   5

Myth 1: The aim of interviewing is to obtain a job offer
   Only half true. The real aim of an interview is to obtain the job *you want.* That often means rejecting job offers you don't want! Incompetent job-seekers, however, become so used to accommodating employers' expecta-   10
tions that they often easily qualify for jobs they don't want. So, before you do back-flips for an employer, be sure you want the job.

Myth 2: Always please the interviewer
   Not true. Try to please yourself. Giving answers that   15
you think will suit a potential employer, losing touch with your own feelings (in order to get in touch with some other person's feelings) and, in general, practicing an abject policy of appeasement are certain to get you nowhere. Of course, don't be hostile – nobody wants to   20
hire someone disagreeable. But there is plainly a middle ground between being too ingratiating and being hostile. An effective interview (whether you are offered the job or not) is like an exciting encounter in conversation with your seatmate on an airplane.   25

Myth 3: Try to control the interview
   Nobody "controls" an interview – neither you nor the interviewer – although one or both parties often try. Then it becomes a phony exchange between two human beings; no business is likely to be transacted. When   30
somebody tries to control us, we resent it. When we try to control somebody, they resent us. Remember, you can't control what employers think of you, just as they can't control what you think of them. So hang loose when interviewing: Never dominate the interview. Com-   35
pulsive behavior turns off your authenticity.

Myth 4: Never interrupt the interviewer
   No dice. "Never talk when I'm interrupting," said McGeorge Bundy.

Good advice.   40
Study the style of effective conversationalists: They
interrupt and are interrupted! An exciting conversation
always makes us feel free – free to interrupt, to disagree,
to agree enthusiastically. We feel comfortable with people who allow us to be natural. So, when interviewing,   45
half the responsibility lies with you. Do you seem uptight? Try being yourself for a change. Employers will
either like or dislike you, but at least you'll have made
an *impression.* Leaving an employer indifferent is the
worst impression you can make. And the way to make   50
an effective impression is to feel free to be yourself,
which frees your interviewers to be *themselves!*

Myth 5: Don't disagree with the interviewer
   Another silly myth. If you don't disagree at times, you
become, in effect, a "yes" man or woman. Don't be afraid   55
to disagree with your interviewer – in an agreeable way.
And don't hesitate to change your mind. The worst that
could happen would be that the interviewer thinks, "There's
a person with an open mind!" The conventional wisdom
says "be yourself," true enough. But how many people   60
can be themselves if they don't feel free to disagree?

myth: something false that most people believe is true   *in touch:* in contact

---

Do you have the main ideas?

Here are eight sentences. Only four of them express important ideas
from the text. The other ideas are in the text, but they are not the
author's main concerns. Choose the four main points, looking back at
the text as often as you want. Then compare answers with some other
students before discussing them with your teacher.

1. A good interview is like an exciting conversation during a journey.
2. Remember that you are trying to find a job that satisfies *you.*
3. Change your mind if you want to.
4. Be yourself.
5. Don't try to dominate the conversation with your interviewer.
6. Try to let interviewers be themselves.
7. Don't be aggressive.
8. Don't be overly respectful of your interviewer.

Guessing words from context

Match each italicized word in column A with one of the meanings in column B. Sometimes you can guess the meaning from the sentence where you find the word; sometimes you will have to look at what comes before and after that sentence. Be careful: There are some extra meanings in column B.

COLUMN A
1. What follows is a list of some of these untruths and some *tips* to help you do your best... (line 4)
2. Giving answers that you think will suit a *potential* employer... (line 16)
3. ...*practicing an abject policy of appeasement*... (lines 18–19)
4. But there is plainly a *middle ground* between being too ingratiating and being hostile. (lines 21–22)
5. When somebody tries to control us, we *resent* it. (line 31)
6. So *hang loose* when interviewing. (line 34)
7. Study the style of *effective* conversationalists... (line 41)
8. Do you seem *uptight?* (lines 46–47)

COLUMN B
a) relax
b) don't telephone often
c) appreciate
d) nervous
e) possible (in the future)
f) model answers
g) powerful
h) successful
i) doing anything to avoid disagreement
j) suggestions
k) a moderate position
l) dislike, feel as unfair
m) the time between two jobs

How will it continue?

How do you think this article will continue? Here are six sentences.
Choose the ones that might logically be used to continue the article.

1. You can never be too quiet in an interview. Employers value people who can listen.
2. Get the help of an employer who has a job you *don't* want: He or she might give you information about finding a job you *do* want.
3. Good job-hunters never tell employers how much they expect to earn: This might make a bad impression.
4. If you aren't sure about what kind of job you want, don't waste time interviewing for jobs now! First find people doing jobs you might want to do and make appointments with them to get more information.
5. Don't cancel appointments to interview even after accepting a job offer you do want. Remember, you are never employed until you are on the payroll.
6. If you don't know the answer to a question, don't say "I don't know." Give what you think is a probable answer: It may be right.

2 How to protect yourself

This is part of a magazine article. Read it carefully, as many times as you want, and don't hesitate to stop to think about what you've read.

At Home

1. *Have a home security checkup.* Ask that a member of your local police department inspect your home and show you which areas are most vulnerable to an intruder. Have him recommend appropriate security devices.

2. *Secure exterior doors and windows.* Replace glass-paned doors with those made of solid wood. Install double-cylinder dead-bolt locks (which must be opened with a key from either side of the door) on all exterior doors, and make sure door hinges have non-removable hinge pins. French doors or other sliding doors that operate on tracks should be made of shatterproof material and kept locked at all times. As an added measure, wedge a broomstick handle on the inside track (cut to fit) – the door will not slide open even if the lock is forced.

Make sure all windows – especially those obscured by bushes – are locked securely. Locking devices vary depending on the type of window. Consult your local hardware store about which kind will be most effective for you. Also, be sure to secure air conditioners so they cannot be pushed in.

3. *Illuminate your home and property.* Position 100-watt bulbs or floodlamps at the front and rear of your home. If you use a side drive or garage, keep these areas brightly lit. Burglars can easily hide out in high shrubbery, so be sure to cut back any bushes near the entrances to your house.

4. *Never open the door to someone you don't know.* Instead, check the caller's identity through a window or door peephole. DO NOT TRUST CHAIN LOCKS – they're easily forced open. If a stranger claims it's an emergency and needs to use your phone, don't be persuaded – tell him to wait outside and place the call *for* him. If he claims to be a delivery or serviceman, ask him to slide his credentials under the door or through the letter box and check thoroughly. Or call his company to verify his identity. Get the phone number from the operator; don't take the one he gives you.

5. *Ask friends to phone before they drop by.* This precaution will save you a lot of anxiety when the doorbell rings. If you live in an apartment, never buzz unidentified persons into your building or let them in when you're entering. If you see a suspicious-looking person in your lobby, don't enter. Call a neighbor to escort you in, or wait for him to leave.

6. *Let friends know when a repairman is coming to your home.* Invite a neighbor over for coffee or have a friend telephone while he's there. If you feel uncomfortable, trust your instincts. Call a friend and pretend you'll be late for a date (let her know there's a stranger in your home) and ask her to call you back in five minutes – giving you the opportunity to ask for help.

7. *If a visitor starts behaving suspiciously or makes a threatening gesture, get out!* Scream FIRE! or POLICE! to attract your neighbors' attention, and run to the nearest public place or neighbor's home. The point is to remove yourself from a potentially dangerous situation at once.

80   8. *Give the impression that someone is home when you go out.* Activate interior lights with timers set to go on and off alternately in different rooms. The sound of a television or radio on in a 85 house or apartment also helps — these can be timer-activated too.

    9. *Engrave valuable items, expensive appliances and tools with an identification number.* Use your driv- 90 er's license or other identifying number and register it with the police. Keep a list of the engraved possessions in your safe-deposit box.

    10. *Don't advertise the fact that you* 95 *live alone.* List only your last name and first initial in the phone directory. Do the same on your mailbox (or list *two* names, giving the impression that you live with a roommate).

    11. *Never give information over the* 100 *phone to an unknown caller.* Instruct your children not to recite your number to a wrong-number caller or give your address over the phone. If you receive a call informing you of some "emer- 105 gency," ask for a number to call back, then hang up and verify the call. A bogus emergency phone call is a common burglar's ruse to get you out of the house.

    12. *If you use a telephone-answer-* 110 *ing machine, never say you are not at home on your recorded message.* Instead say, "You have reached the Browns' residence, but we are unable to talk with you just now." 115

Summary skills

Here are some pictures illustrating the text. Each one corresponds to one of the numbered instructions in the text, but they are not in order. Match numbers and pictures. Be careful: Some numbers will have no picture.

a   b   c

d   e

f   g

Guessing words from context

Find single words in the text that seem to correspond to the definitions given below.

Example (in lines 1–6): unwanted visitor
Answer: intruder

Now find words for these meanings in lines 1–29:
1. broken open
2. hidden
3. attach tightly

Find words for these meanings in lines 30–61:
4. small trees
5. something you can see out of without being seen
6. identification papers
7. entrance hall of apartment building
8. telephone (verb)

Find words for these meanings in lines 87–115:
9. mark by cutting letters or numbers into
10. false

Making connections

Misunderstandings sometimes happen because we do not realize which person or thing is meant by a word like *she* or *this*. This exercise will give you practice in making connections between words like these and their meanings.

Give the meaning of each word or phrase in italics. The meaning may be in the same sentence or somewhere else in the text.

Example (in line 5): Have *him* recommend appropriate security devices.
Answer: Him means a member of your local police department.

1. ... keep *these areas* brightly lit. (line 34)
2. ... don't take the one *he* gives you. (line 52)
3. ... wait for *him* to leave. (line 61)
4. ... while *he's* there. (line 65)
5. ... ask *her* to call you back ... (line 69)
6. ... register *it* with the police. (line 91)

Why?

You will probably want to look back at the text to find the answers to some of these questions, and you will need to think about the text.

1. Why should you illuminate your house and property?
2. Why should you ask for deliverymen's credentials?
3. Why shouldn't you enter your lobby if there is a suspicious-looking person there?
4. Why should you give the impression that someone is home when you go out?
5. Why should you engrave valuable items with an identification number?
6. Why shouldn't you give your address over the phone?

3 How to save a life

Here are some instructions for resuscitation, or artificial respiration – helping someone start breathing again when they have stopped. Read the instructions, stopping as often as you want. Feel free to read them more than once.

HOW TO CARRY OUT RESUSCITATION

Mouth-to-mouth resuscitation is the easiest form of artificial respiration for the layman to apply and should be used in almost all circumstances except when there is severe injury to the face and mouth, when the casualty is pinned in a face-down position, or if vomiting occurs as breathing is re-established and interferes with resuscitation.   5

If a casualty is not breathing:

1   Make sure the air passages are not obstructed. Pull the head firmly back as far as it will go, bringing the lower jaw upward and forward until the front teeth meet. In this position   10 the tongue cannot fall back and block the throat. Remove any solid or fluid blockage, scooping it out with the fingers if necessary and blotting up blood or vomit from the mouth with a handkerchief or tissue. This may be sufficient to restart breathing. This is a vital step, as without clearing the air   15 passage there is no point going on to the next stage.

2   Cover the patient's mouth with yours and pinch the nose to keep it closed. Blow. Watch the patient's chest for movement. Remove your mouth, inhale, replace your mouth and blow again. Expel air deeply and slowly. Make sure that you have   20 an airtight seal so that air does not escape as you blow.

3   If the chest does not rise and fall, check to make sure that the head position is correct.

With babies and young children cover both nose and mouth with your mouth. If you do not relish such close contact with   25 the patient, place a clean handkerchief over the casualty's (nose and) mouth and breathe through it.

Summary skills 1

Put one word in each blank on the flow chart. Look back at the text as
often as you want.

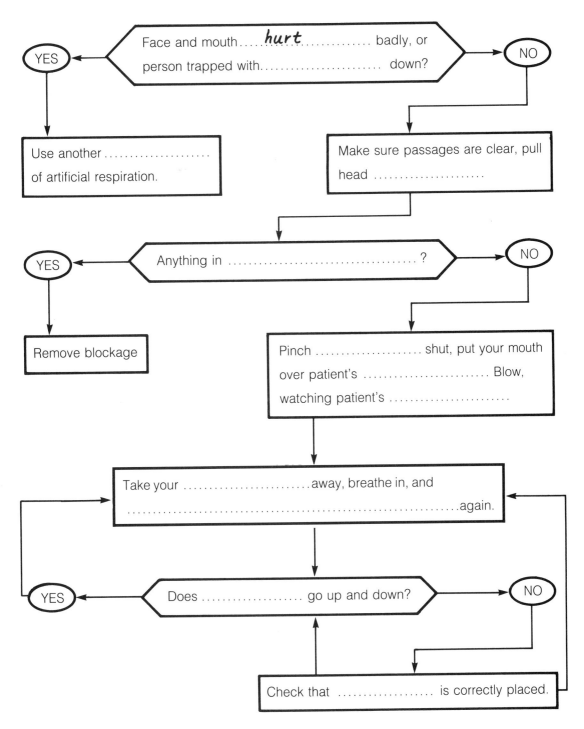

Face and mouth.....*hurt*.............. badly, or
person trapped with...................... down?

YES

NO

Use another ....
of artificial respiration.

Make sure passages are clear, pull
head ....

Anything in ....?

YES

NO

Remove blockage

Pinch .... shut, put your mouth
over patient's .... Blow,
watching patient's ....

Take your ....away, breathe in, and
....again.

YES

NO

Does .... go up and down?

Check that .... is correctly placed.

11

Summary skills 2

Put the pictures into the correct order. Look back at the text if you
want.

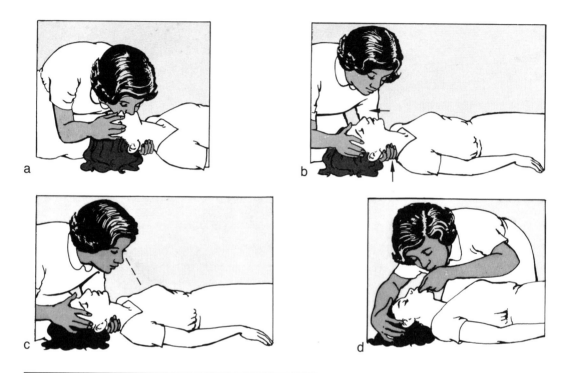

Guessing words from context

Match each word in italics in column A with the meaning in column B
that comes closest to it. Column B has some extra meanings.

COLUMN A

1. ...easiest form of artifical respiration for the
   layman to apply...(line 2)
2. ...for the layman to *apply*...(line 2)
3. ...when there is *severe* injury...(line 3)
4. ...when the casualty is *pinned* in a face-down
   position,...(line 4)
5. If a *casualty* is not breathing:...(line 7)
6. ...the air passages are not *obstructed*. (line 8)
7. ...*scooping* it out with the fingers...(line 12)
8. *Expel* air deeply and slowly. (line 20)
9. If you do not *relish* such close contact...(line 25)

COLUMN B

a) lying
b) trapped
c) use
d) like the idea of
e) very bad
f) push out
g) small
h) non-specialist
i) remember
j) injured person
k) taking
l) blocked
m) have

Vocabulary links

Part of our understanding of a text is based on recognition of the links between words – words that mean the same as each other, that relate to parts of the same thing, and so on. Do this exercise about vocabulary links in the text.

1. Find two words that mean *the person who is not breathing without help*.
2. Find the names of two *air passages* (line 8).
3. Find three other words or expressions that have to do with *removing things from the mouth* (line 11).
4. Find the names of two parts of the face and mouth.
5. Find one word and one expression that mean the same as *blow* (line 21).

4 How to win at marriage

This is part of an article from a women's magazine. Read the text carefully, stopping as often as you want. Imagine you have to write a summary of the text. Then do the exercises, looking back at the text as often as you wish. Remember, the exercises are to teach you, not test you.

1   Marriage is war. Let's get that straight, first of all.

To those currently married, this will hardly be news. The news is that the war is winnable,
5   and it doesn't have to be hell.

How can you win? You win by not winning; let's say that, first. But maybe we should have said, first of all, by not losing. That's what women have to learn. To keep it up, to fight
10   again, not to be beaten, not to destroy; that's what marriage is. Don't expect to win – but expect not to lose. This will make you magnanimous, and unafraid.

15   **How To Fight – the Ground Rules**
Fight about whatever comes along. Don't scorn to do battle over nothing. Most
20   battles are over nothing. Every small fight is about some big issue. Likewise, every big fight takes its form from some unimportant
25   matter.

Fights in front of an audience don't count. Then you're not fighting, you're performing. Tell the kids to go out-
30   side or in the other room, you and Daddy want to fight now. And you'll find that your friends and relatives are more relieved than disappointed
35   when you stop requiring their presence at your private quarrels.

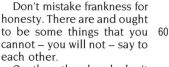
Culver Pictures, Inc.

Screaming and yelling are nice if you're the type who can bring that sort of thing off. I can't. When I yell, I get madder. Some people get
40   less mad by yelling. Let them yell. Don't consider decibels as an index of anything.

On the other hand, don't try to sound reasonable. "You know," in a calm, measured tone, "that when you do that it's very upsetting to
45   me" is not a decent way for a fighter to talk. You don't have to be histrionic, but you should at least sound irritated.

Cry, if you like. But be sure you're not crying out of a failure to say what you mean. Say what you mean, as clearly and lengthily as you can.
50   Then cry. Or if you start crying, don't stop talking.

Violence is an admission of defeat. Don't hit him. (I mean don't hit him *at all* – no "playful" slaps. These are sneaky, unfair, and as-
55   sume you're either a child or his mother.) If he hits you, walk out. He just lost.

Don't mistake frankness for honesty. There are and ought to be some things that you
60   cannot – you will not – say to each other.

On the other hand, don't mistake the figurative for the irremediable. I think you are
65   an arrogant, egotistical, cold, selfish liar – well, that can go by. I'm talking about a big, serious, once-every-three-to-
70   five-years fight here, you understand. If you find yourselves talking to each other this way regularly, you don't like each other, which is the best of all reasons for divorce.
75   And don't tolerate (or make) threats to leave. If he tries this, point the door out to him. And if *he's* done something bad enough to
80   leave him for, don't threaten him with "next time." Go.

Refusal to fight, or to continue fighting, is an act of cowardice as well as a breach of courtesy that cannot be tolerated, like walking
85   off the court in the middle of the game. You have to go on with it, out of courtesy, till your opponent is as bored as you are, and ready to stop, even if you're just going through the motions.
90   Once you both get tired of it, let it wind down. Then go to your separate corners. Get away from each other for a while, and don't

consider that as punishment of the other per-
95 son. You just had a fight, right now you hate
each other; impose an hour of silence, take a
walk, go in another room. Slam doors on the
way.

Remember: you're fighting because you love
100 each other. You're mad at each other because
you love each other. If you didn't love each
other, you wouldn't have to fight. One of you
could walk out. Don't take it as evidence that
he doesn't love you. You know you still love
105 him, though at the moment you happen to
hate him.

Make it up however you choose. But – this
is important – don't make or expect apologies.

Unless something irremediable has been said,
there is no need for them. At the next natural 110
encounter, you should be able to start somewhere else, on something new.

And with good grace and friendship. If you're
still mad after five or six hours, you didn't fight
hard enough in the first place, and you'll have 115
to do it over again, and this time try to get it
right.

One other thing about making up: never do
it in bed. You ought to make friends again
before you make love. Otherwise sex becomes 120
a power play, and dishonest – a way of de-
nying your differences rather than accepting
them.

magnanimous: generous
screaming and yelling: shouting
irremediable: impossible to correct
make it up: become friendly again, after an argument

Summary skills

Complete this table. Look back at the text as often as you want.

Do	Don't	
1.	✓	think you can win.
2. ✓		fight about small things, if you want to.
3.		fight when other people are with you.
4.		yell if it makes you madder.
5.		let your partner know how angry you are.
6.		stop fighting to cry.
7.		say you're going to leave your partner.
8.		continue fighting until you're both ready to stop.
9.		stay away from each other for a while after fighting.
10.		forget that you love one another.
11.		say you're sorry.
12.		be friendly if you are still angry after the fight.
13.		make love before you have both stopped being angry.

Guessing words from context

Three things can help you guess words you don't know:
– what you find in the text,
– what you know about similar words, and
– what you know about the world.
Guess the probable meaning of each word.

1. *scorn* (line 18): From the other sentences in this paragraph, you
   know the author thinks that it is all right for people to fight over
   small things. So *scorn* probably means _____.
2. *relieved* (line 34): This must have a meaning that can be opposed to
   disappointed; so perhaps it means _____.
3. *sneaky* (line 55): Is it good or bad to be sneaky?
4. *cowardice* (line 84): Is cowardice a good or bad character trait?
5. *wind down* (lines 91–92): Does this mean stop suddenly or come to
   an end slowly?

Now guess the meanings of these three words:
6. *currently* (line 3)
7. *issue* (line 22)
8. *requiring* (line 35)

"This argument isn't settled until you argue back!"

Vocabulary links

Recognizing which words have related meanings in a text can help your understanding of it. Answer these questions about words that are linked.

1. *unimportant* (line 24): Find two words in this paragraph that mean *unimportant*, or *an unimportant thing*.
2. *audience* (line 26): Find three words in this paragraph that refer to an audience.
3. *reasonable* (line 42): Find four words in this paragraph that mean the same or the opposite of this word.
4. *violence* (line 53): Find two examples of violent actions in this paragraph.

How will it continue?

How do you think this article will continue? Here are five sentences. Choose the ones that might reasonably be in the rest of the article.

1. Don't fight about religion. No one should marry expecting to convert the other.
2. Don't fight about what he did three years ago (if he's stopped doing it since). Forget three years ago.
3. Don't fight if he's obviously under big pressure from his work or some other area of his life that has nothing to do with your marriage.
4. Accept no limits as to the "subject under discussion." You can discuss whatever you want. It's not a committee meeting, it's a domestic quarrel.
5. Try to finish each fight by making some kind of agreement about how you will change your behavior in the future.

Part 2   Descriptions: What things are like

5   Athens is dying

Read this news article about the problems of Athens. Read it carefully, as many times as you want, before beginning the questions. Look back at it while you are doing the exercises: They are meant to help you, not to test your memory.

Stinking buses, their passengers pale and tired, jam the crowded streets. Drivers shout at one another and honk their horns. Smog smarts
5 the eyes and chokes the senses. The scene is Athens at rush hour. The city of Plato and Pericles is a sorry state of affairs, built without a plan, lacking even adequate sewerage facilities,
10 hemmed in by mountains and the sea, its 135 square miles crammed with 3.7 million people. Even Athens' ruins are in ruin: sulfur dioxide eats away at the marble of the Parthenon
15 and other treasures on the Acropolis. As Greek Premier Constantine Karamanlis has said, ''The only solution for Athens would be to demolish half of it and start all over again.''
20 So great has been the population flow toward the city that entire hinterland villages stand vacant or nearly so. About 120,000 people from outlying provinces move to Athens every year,
25 with the result that 40% of Greece's citizenry are now packed into the capital. The migrants come for the few available jobs, which are usually no better than the ones they fled. At the
30 current rate of migration, Athens by the year 2000 will have a population of 6.5 million, more than half the nation.
Aside from overcrowding and poor public transport, the biggest problems
35 confronting Athenians are noise and pollution. A government study concluded that Athens was the noisiest city in the world. Smog is almost at killing

levels: 180–300 mg of sulfur dioxide per cubic meter of air, or up to four 40 times the level that the World Health Organization considers safe. Nearly half the pollution comes from cars. Despite high prices for vehicles and fuel ($2.95 per gallon), nearly 100,000 automo- 45 biles are sold in Greece each year; 3,000 driver's licenses are issued in Athens monthly.
After decades of neglect, Athens is at last getting some attention. In March 50 a committee of representatives from all major public service ministries met to discuss a plan to unclog the city, make it livable and clean up its environment. A save-Athens ministry, which will 55 soon begin functioning, will propose

heavy taxes to discourage in-migration, a minimum of $5 billion in public spending for Athens alone, and other projects for the countryside to encourage residents to stay put. A master plan that will move many government offices to the city's fringes is already in the works. Meanwhile, more Greeks keep moving into Athens. With few parks and precious few oxygen-producing plants, the city and its citizens are literally suffocating.

stinking: smelling very bad, having a very unpleasant odor
sewerage: a system that moves the human waste from toilets out of the city, to a place where it
   is treated chemically
unclog the city: stop it from being so crowded

Summary skills

Choose one subject from the following list of topics discussed in the text. Then read the text, making brief notes on this page about the subject you have chosen. It is not necessary to write complete sentences.

When you have finished your notes, find one or two other people in the class who have chosen the same subject as you. Compare your notes and write a new set of notes that you agree on.

1. Air pollution
2. Overcrowding
3. Traffic

Guessing words from context

Three things can help you guess words you do not know:
– what you find in the text,
– what you know about similar words, and
– what you know about the world.
Guess the probable meaning of each word.

1. *lacking* (line 8): This sentence describes the problems of Athens; so
   "lacking adequate sewerage facilities" probably means ⎯⎯⎯⎯⎯⎯⎯
   adequate sewerage facilities.
2. *crammed* (line 11): Because this is a sentence about Athens' problems,
   3.7 million people is probably considered a lot of people
   for 135 square miles. So *crammed* probably means ⎯⎯⎯⎯⎯⎯⎯⎯⎯.
3. *fled* (line 29): The new jobs in Athens are usually no better than the
   old jobs the migrants ⎯⎯⎯⎯⎯⎯⎯.
4. *confronting* (line 35): "The problems confronting Athenians" are the
   problems that Athenians ⎯⎯⎯⎯⎯⎯⎯.
5. *decades* (line 49): It is not easy to guess exactly what this word
   means, but "at last" tells you that it means ⎯⎯⎯⎯⎯⎯⎯⎯⎯.
6. *stay put* (line 61): This means not to ⎯⎯⎯⎯⎯⎯⎯.
7. *is already in the works* (lines 63–64): This means has already ⎯⎯⎯⎯⎯⎯⎯.

"I know what – let's stay in and get some fresh air."

Facts and figures

Find the information in the text that will help you solve these
mathematical problems. You may want to work with a partner.

1. Complete this graph about Athens' growing population. Put a dot
   wherever you know what Athens' future population will be. Then
   connect the dots.

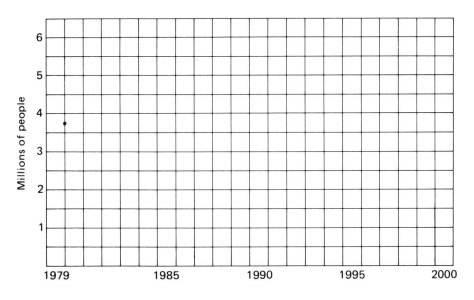

2. How many driver's licenses are issued in Athens every year?
3. How many people per square mile were living in Athens when the
   article was written?
4. What is the present population of Greece?
5. What is the level of sulfur dioxide considered safe by the World
   Health Organization?

21

6 Zen and the art of motorcycle maintenance

This text is the beginning of the first chapter in a book called *Zen and the Art of Motorcycle Maintenance*. Every 15 lines or so you will find a short summary of what you have just read. But the summary has mistakes in it! Cross out the mistaken words or phrases in the summary and write the correct ones; or, on a separate piece of paper, write down the mistakes and corrections.

Example: This is the ~~last~~ **first** part of a novel.

I can see by my watch, without taking my hand from the left grip of the cycle, that it is eight-thirty in the morning. The wind, even at sixty miles an hour, is warm and humid. When it's this hot and muggy at eight-thirty, I'm wondering what it's going to be like   5
in the afternoon.

In the wind are pungent odors from the marshes by the road. We are in an area of the Central Plains filled with thousands of duck hunting sloughs, heading northwest from Minneapolis toward the Dakotas. This   10
highway is an old concrete two-laner that hasn't had much traffic since a four-laner went in parallel to it several years ago. When we pass a marsh the air suddenly becomes cooler. Then, when we are past, it suddenly warms up again.   15

Summary 1

The narrator is traveling across an area of the Rocky Mountains by motorcycle. It is a hot, dry morning, and there are a lot of hills along the new highway the narrator is using. The air from the marshes is warm.

I'm happy to be riding back into this country. It is a kind of nowhere, famous for nothing at all and has an appeal because of just that. Tensions disappear along old roads like this. We bump along the beat-up concrete between the cattails and stretches of meadow and then   20

---

odors: smells
marshes: areas of low, wet, soft land
concrete: building material used for road surfaces

narrator: the person who is telling the story
meadow: grassland

more cattails and marsh grass. Here and there is a
stretch of open water and if you look closely you can
see wild ducks at the edge of the cattails. And turtles.
...There's a red-winged blackbird.

    I whack Chris's knee and point to it.   25

    "What!" he hollers.

    "Blackbird!"

    He says something I don't hear. "What?" I holler
back.

    He grabs the back of my helmet and hollers up,   30
"I've seen *lots* of those, Dad!"

Summary 2

This is the first time the narrator has been in this country. He is unhappy to

be back in this irritating place and see the plants and animals again. His

son, Chris, who is riding beside him on another cycle, is impressed with the

bird his dad notices.

    "Oh!" I holler back. Then I nod. At age eleven you
don't get very impressed with red-winged blackbirds.

    You have to get older for that. For me this is all
mixed with memories that he doesn't have. Cold morn- 35
ings long ago when the marsh grass had turned brown
and cattails were waving in the northwest wind. The
pungent smell then was from muck stirred up by hip
boots while we were getting in position for the sun to
come up and the duck season to open. Or winters when 40
the sloughs were frozen over and dead and I could walk
across the ice and snow between the dead cattails and
see nothing but grey skies and dead things and cold.
The blackbirds were gone then. But now in July they're
back and everything is at its alivest and every foot of 45
these sloughs is humming and cricking and buzzing
and chirping, a whole community of millions of living
things living out their lives in a kind of benign
continuum.

Summary 3

Chris is 11; the narrator thinks that is too old to be impressed with

blackbirds. The blackbird is interesting to the narrator because it reminds

him of a story he read: deer hunting in the marshes in the autumn, walking

through the mud in the winter.

---

benign: having a kind or gentle nature

You see things vacationing on a motorcycle in a   50
way that is completely different from any other. In a
car you're always in a compartment, and because you're
used to it you don't realize that through that car window everything you see is just more TV. You're a pas-
sive observer and it is all moving by you boringly in a   55
frame.

On a cycle the frame is gone. You're completely in
contact with it all. You're *in* the scene, not just watching it anymore, and the sense of presence is overwhelm-
ing. That concrete whizzing by five inches below your   60
foot is the real thing, the same stuff you walk on, it's
right there, so blurred you can't focus on it, yet you can
put your foot down and touch it anytime, and the whole
thing, the whole experience, is never removed from
immediate consciousness.   65

Chris and I are traveling to Montana with some
friends riding up ahead, and maybe headed farther than
that. Plans are deliberately indefinite, more to travel
than to arrive anywhere. We are just vacationing.

Summary 4

Traveling on a motorcycle is not so good as traveling by car, because on a

motorcycle you are a participant rather than a spectator. You can ignore

the experience of traveling. The narrator and his son have very definite

plans about their vacation, because it is the destination that interests them

more than the journey.

---

blurred: when something is blurred you cannot see it clearly   *deliberately:* not accidentally

Do you have the main ideas?

Which three of the following subjects do you think the author is most interested in discussing in this passage?

– How to hunt ducks.
– The scenery.
– The narrator's relationship with his son, Chris.
– The narrator's past experience of this place.
– The pleasure and interest of traveling by motorcycle.
– The weather.
– Chris's attitude to nature.

Guessing words from context

Find *single* words in the text that seem to correspond to the definitions given below.

Example (in lines 1–5): The part of a motorcycle that you hold in your hand when the cycle is moving.
Answer: grip

Now find words for these meanings in lines 1–25:
 1. A muddy place where people go to hunt ducks.
 2. A road wide enough for two cars side by side.
 3. Wet, close, heavy (referring to the weather).
 4. Plants that grow in wet places, whose flowers look like the tails of cats.
 5. Move over a rough road, for example, in a car or on a cycle.

Find words for these meanings in lines 26–49:
 6. Soft, wet mud mixed with dead plants.
 7. The protective hat a motorcyclist wears.
 8. Shouts.

Find words for these meanings in lines 50–69:
 9. Adjust your eyes (or a camera) so the image is clear.
10. Speeding.
11. Making you feel powerless.

7 Vacationing in Mexico

Here is part of a tourist brochure. Read it carefully, stopping to think if you want. You can read it more than once.

Each year more travelers are finding their way to the sun coasts of Mexico; where ancient civilizations once honored the sun, modern sun worshippers are discovering superb vacation destinations. Airlines now schedule weekly flights from major national and international points to a variety of sun coast resort areas. 5

The peninsula of **Baja California** provides one of the most splendid vacation sites in the Western Hemisphere. The peninsula is divided into two states: Baja California Norte and Baja California Sur, which are now connected 10 by the **Benito Juárez Trans-peninsular Highway**, so that the entire peninsula can be easily reached by car, as well as by sea and air. A chain of new hotels offer deluxe accommodations, but there are also numerous camping grounds, trailer parks and wayside inns for those who 15 prefer casual-living vacations. At the southern end of the peninsula, **La Paz, San José del Cabo** and **Cabo San Lucas** offer rapidly expanding deluxe facilities to accommodate the growing influx of visitors. All have good accommodations, restaurants, sports facilities and meeting 20 rooms. In addition, La Paz, with its duty-free zone, is a shopper's paradise.

Kino Bay, a coastal resort on the mainland near Hermosillo, is expanding and will soon offer new luxurious tourist accommodations. 25

South along the coast are **Topolobampo** and **Los Mochis**, the former a ferry terminus serving La Paz on the Peninsula, and boasting the largest natural bay in the world; and the latter a starting point for the Chihuahua-Pacific Railway trip which goes through the breathtaking 30 Copper Canyon to the city of Chihuahua.

Mazatlán, the sailfish capital of the world, has developed a large new resort complex to accommodate its many visitors. Famous for its jumbo shrimp and other delicious seafood, Mazatlán also offers seasonal bullfights, 35 lively evening entertainment and big-game fishing. An international fishing tournament is held there each fall. Modern convention and sports facilities are available.

Mazatlán is easily reached from other major cities by good
highways and an international airport.   40
   Puerto Vallarta, once a sleepy fishing village, is now
one of Mexico's fastest growing resorts. The red-tiled
roofs and cobblestoned streets contrast with the luxurious
new hotels. The annual temperature averages around
80°F., offering a perfect climate for parasailing, skin   45
diving, surfing and other aquatic sports. Evening
entertainment includes seafood dinners, floor shows and
disco dancing that lasts until daybreak. Big-game hunting
and fishing are also popular within this region of coastal
Mexico.   50

Getting the picture

Look through the text, and find the name of each numbered place on
the map.

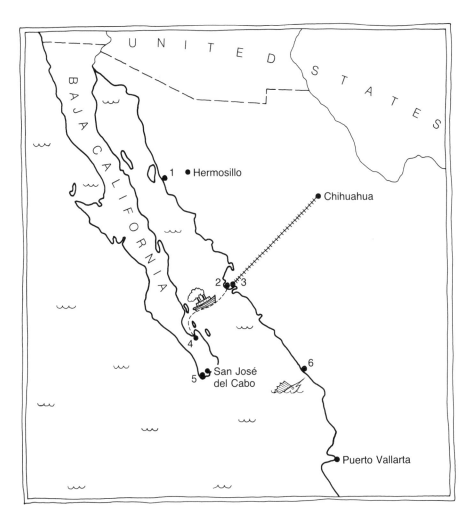

Reading for specific information

Suggest places where the following people might stay, by referring back to the information in the text. Sometimes more than one place may be appropriate.

1. A couple in their forties who want to see some typical Mexican entertainment, eat well, and do some fishing.
2. A firm of New York lawyers looking for a place to hold a big three-day business meeting. A convenient airport is essential. Tennis and squash courts are desirable.
3. A man in his sixties who wants to spend a relaxed holiday seeing nice scenery; he enjoys train trips.
4. A family with three small children who want to camp in pleasant surroundings.
5. A 25-year-old engineer who wants two weeks of sun and water sports and an opportunity to meet other young people for dancing and other entertainment.

Guessing words from context

Match each word in italics in column A with the meaning in column B
that comes closest to it. Column B has some extra meanings.

COLUMN A
1. ...a variety of sun coast *resort* areas. (line 6)
2. ...those who prefer *casual*-living vacations. (line 16)
3. ...*big-game* fishing. (line 36)
4. Modern *convention* and sports facilities are available. (line 38)
5. ...sports *facilities* are available. (line 38)
6. The red-tiled roofs and *cobblestoned* streets... (line 43)
7. ...parasailing, skin diving, surfing and other *aquatic* sports. (line 46)
8. ...disco dancing that lasts until *daybreak*. (line 48)

COLUMN B
a) large fish
b) water
c) religious
d) large meeting
e) lively
f) relaxed
g) sunrise
h) rooms and equipment
i) vacation
j) old-fashioned
k) competitive
l) lively

8   Men of the Pine Barrens

These are descriptions of two men who live in the Pine Barrens in New Jersey. Very few people make their homes in this forest area, but it is only a day's drive from several million people. The narrator has stopped at a stranger's house to ask for a glass of water.

I called out to ask if anyone was home, and a voice called back, "Come in. Come in. Come on the hell in."

I walked through a vestibule that had a dirt floor, stepped up into a kitchen, and went on into another 5
room that had several overstuffed chairs in it and a porcelain-topped table, where Fred Brown was seated, eating a pork chop. He was dressed in a white sleeveless shirt, ankle-top shoes, and undershorts. He gave me a cheerful greeting and, without asking 10
why I had come or what I wanted, picked up a pair of khaki trousers that had been tossed onto one of the overstuffed chairs and asked me to sit down. He set the trousers on another chair, and he apologized for being in the middle of his breakfast, explaining 15
that he seldom drank much but the night before he had had a few drinks and this had caused his day to start slowly. "I don't know what's the matter with me, but there's got to be something the matter with me, because drink don't agree with me anymore," 20
he said. He had a raw onion in one hand, and while he talked he shaved slices from the onion and ate them between bites of the chop. He was a muscular and well-built man, with short, bristly white hair, and he had bright, fast-moving eyes in a wide-open 25
face. His legs were trim and strong, with large muscles in the calves. I guessed that he was about sixty and for a man of sixty he seemed to be in remarkably good shape. He was actually seventy-nine. "My rule is: Never eat except when you're hungry," he said, 30
and he ate another slice of the onion.

In a straight-backed chair near the doorway to the kitchen sat a young man with long black hair, who

wore a visored red leather cap that had darkened
with age. His shirt was coarse-woven and had eyelets   35
down a V neck that was laced with a thong. His
trousers were made of canvas, and he was wearing
gum boots. His arms were folded, his legs were
stretched out, he had one ankle over the other, and
as he sat there he appeared to be sighting carefully   40
past his feet, as if his toes were the outer frame of
a gunsight and he could see some sort of target in
the floor. When I had entered, I had said hello to
him, and he had nodded without looking up. He
had a long, straight nose and high cheekbones, in   45
a deeply tanned face that was, somehow, gaunt. I
had no idea whether he was shy or hostile. Even-
tually, when I came to know him, I found him to
be as shy a person as I have ever had a chance to
know.   50

Reading for specific information

Complete this table. The first row is done for you as an example.

	Fred Brown	*The young man*
age	79; looks 60	doesn't say
hair		
eyes		
face		
shirt		
trousers		
legs		
shoes		
personality		

Guessing words from context

Match each word in italics in column A with the meaning in column B that comes closest to it. Column B has some extra meanings.

COLUMN A
1. I walked through a *vestibule* ... (line 4)
2. ... another room that had several *overstuffed* chairs ... (line 6)
3. ... trousers that had been *tossed* onto one of the overstuffed chairs ... (line 12)
4. His legs were *trim* and strong, ... (line 26)
5. ... with large muscles in the *calves*. (line 27)
6. ... a V neck that was laced with a *thong*. (line 36)
7. His trousers were made of *canvas*, ... (line 37)
8. ... he could see some sort of *target* ... (line 42)
9. ... whether he was shy or *hostile*. (line 47)

COLUMN B
a) put carefully
b) a kind of cotton material
c) big and soft
d) very unfriendly
e) thrown
f) something you try to shoot
g) arms
h) not fat
i) lower parts of the legs
j) small entrance hall
k) long, thin piece of leather
l) bit of forest
m) dirty

Inference

Sometimes you can find information in a text that is not stated clearly in the words there. You infer the information – that is, you make a logical guess – either from what is in the text or by using your knowledge of the world, or both.

   Try to infer the probable answers to these questions by looking at the text; be ready to give your reasons.

1. What is the weather like?
2. Are there many tourists in the Pine Barrens?
3. Does Fred Brown work for anyone besides himself?
4. Does Fred walk much?
5. What general type of work does the young man do?
6. Who had gotten up first that morning, Fred or the young man?

Part 3   Processes: How things happen

9 Power

Reading for specific information

On the next page there is a newspaper article in which a psychologist talks about power and how it affects people. Before reading the article, look at the table below and try to complete it as quickly as you can by looking at the article. Don't read the whole article now; just look for the parts of the article that will help you complete the table. Write "Yes," "No," or "DS" (if the text doesn't say). The first item is done for you as an example.

	People who need and have power	*People who need power but don't have it*
Mentally healthy	*yes*	*no*
Depressed		
Sexually satisfied		
Self-assured		
Good judges of sincerity		
Loyal friends		
Attractive to the opposite sex		
Wise		

33

Now read the article carefully, more than once if you wish, and stop as often as you want.

How much do you know about people and how they handle positions of power? Some individuals can handle it; others cannot. Test your knowledge by answering the following questions true or false.

1) Most people who need, or have, power are emotionally disturbed.
2) Power is one of the best anti-depressants known.
3) A desire for power usually has a negative effect on sex.
4) Those who have a high need for power are usually self-assured and are able to dismiss flattery.
5) Americans are more confused in their feelings regarding power than are most other peoples.
6) When people become powerful or successful they often seek new friends.
7) Both men and women are attracted to power in members of the opposite sex.
8) The belief that "power corrupts" has little basis in fact.

ANSWERS

1) FALSE. Individuals who have unusually high needs for power and do not have it are apt to be emotionally disturbed. Harvey Rich, a Washington psychoanalyst who has examined many people who do have power, found that most of them were healthy, adjusted and relatively trouble-free.

2) TRUE. Power seems to give most people a tremendous lift. While it may create a lot of stress, a lack of power creates a lot more. Dr. Bertram Brown, a psychiatrist and former head of the National Institute of Mental Health, says that exercising power is the most effective short-range anti-depressant in the world.

3) TRUE. If the drive for power isn't being fulfilled in other ways, it can have a disastrous effect on sex. Sex, in itself, can be used as a weapon of power in a marriage, and the need for power is a factor in most rapes.

4) FALSE. Eugene Fodor, a professor of psychology at Clarkson University, found that people who are high in the need for power are also high in the need for ingratiation, and are likely to reward those who flatter them.

5) TRUE. As David McClelland, Harvard professor of psychology, points out, Americans are heavily influenced by religious values that exalt lowly status. They are influenced by political values that stress equality and the need for strong checks on power.

6) TRUE. Powerful people frequently are tempted to drop old friends in favor of those who are more powerful. They prefer to socialize with those of equal or superior power.

7) FALSE. Men are not usually attracted to powerful women. More often, they feel threatened by them. Women, however, find men with power much more attractive than those without it. When the man loses power, he almost immediately becomes less sexually attractive to women. Henry Kissinger, former U.S. secretary of state, called power the great aphrodisiac.

8) FALSE. The facts indicate that in most cases, power still corrupts. One of the reasons is that the powerful tend to believe those who try to make their way up the ladder through flattery. This susceptibility to flattery stands in the way of the ability to see reality and to make wise decisions. Power still tends to destroy itself.

flattery: untrue compliments
corrupts: makes people evil
rapes: forced sexual intercourse

Guessing words from context

Here is a list of words and expressions from the text. Choose an appropriate word or expression for each blank in the sentences. You will not use all the words.

dismiss (line 14)   fulfilled (line 43)
peoples (line 17)   weapon (line 45)
relatively (line 32)   ingratiation (line 52)
lift (line 34)   status (line 57)
short-range (line 40)

1. Give yourself _____ goals so you can see that you're making progress.
2. Engineers earn more money and have higher _____ in America than in England.
3. I was a little depressed earlier in the week, but seeing my cousin again gave me a real _____.
4. I thought she might be lying, but then I had to _____ the idea.
5. What type of _____ was used to kill the man?
6. The _____ of western Europe are very different from those of Asia.
7. Most of her needs were _____ by her job and her family.

Reading carefully for details

You may want to look back at the text while answering these questions. Write **T** if the sentence is true according to the text, **F** if the sentence is false according to the text, and **DS** if the text doesn't say.

1. Many powerful people go to Harvey Rich with emotional problems.
2. Exercising regularly is one way to combat depression caused by too much power.
3. Most men who rape do it to feel powerful.
4. People who need power tend to choose employees who don't.
5. Religious and political values in America discourage people from trying to become powerful.
6. If you want powerful people to like you, say they're better than they are.

10 Smoke signals

Here is a magazine article about children who started fires. Read it as many times as you want. Feel free to stop to think about what you have read.

While working as a volunteer with the San Francisco Fire Department in 1980, Pamela McClaughlin noticed some interesting statistics: Of the roughly 2,000 fires started in San Francisco each year, more than half were started by boys under the age of 18. One boy set small fires in his grandmother's bedroom; another burned off all the sleeves of the shirts in his closet. An overweight youngster had tried lighting fires in the family's refrigerator.

In most cases records indicated that the boys were without a strong father figure in their lives. McClaughlin wondered if the fires were signals for help and could be prevented by connecting the boys with friendly firemen on a one-to-one basis. The firemen could provide some needed guidance in more ways than one.

It took McClaughlin two months of traveling from fire station to fire station to get 20 volunteers who then underwent three training sessions with a psychologist before beginning their new responsibilities. The boys were referred by schools and social agencies.

Now a national foundation, the Firehawk program has had a 100 percent success rate: None of the 60 or so boys who have been paired with a fireman for a year or longer have been known to set fires again.

"Firehawk works because these kids need attention," says fireman Craig Brown. "The kid knows I'm serious. I call him, take him to ball games, and we talk about fire prevention at the firehouse where he can see what it takes to prevent fires. The first month we snap him to attention, and slowly a bond is created, and he starts calling me because he knows I want him to survive and do well in life."

Through their involvement with the firemen, the boys learn firsthand about the dangers of fire – especially in relation to someone they care about. One of Brown's charges, a 7-year-old who had been setting fires since he was 4, was very upset when Brown, after fighting a three-alarm fire, canceled a planned get-together. "I was groggy from the effects of carbon monoxide, and I had pneumonia," Brown says. "The boy had no idea what a fire could do to somebody, and it was me telling him. His mother said he worried for three days."

Dr. Jessica Gaynor, a family psychologist and executive director of Firehawk, maintains contact with all the boys even

36

after they have outgrown their companion firemen.

80   "We are not working with child arsonists," she says. "We are working with children who are becoming involved in fire- setting behavior. This is an im- portant distinction because the juvenile justice system is ready 85 to call them arsonists. We are an early intervention program that keeps kids out of the system."

Summary skills

Here is a chart of the main events in the process of helping the young boys. Some events are labeled and some are not. Put in the missing labels.

1. _____

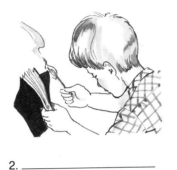

2. _____
   _____

3. Referral to fireman volunteer

4. Boy learns about fire prevention

5. Boy goes out with fireman

6. _____
   _____

7. _____
   _____

Guessing words from context

Match each word in italics in column A with the meaning in column B
that comes closest to it. Column B has some extra meanings.

COLUMN A

1. An *overweight* youngster had tried lighting fires
   ... (lines 12–13)
2. In most cases records *indicated* ... (lines 16–17)
3. The firemen could provide some needed *guidance*
   ... (line 25)
4. The boys were *referred* by schools ... (line 34)
5. ... known to *set* fires again. (line 41)
6. ... slowly a *bond* is created ... (line 52)
7. ... the boys learn *firsthand* about the dangers of
   fire ... (line 58)
8. One of Brown's *charges*, a 7-year-old ... (line 61)
9. "I was *groggy* from the effects of carbon
   monoxide ... " (line 66)
10. ... even after they have *outgrown* their
    companion firemen. (line 77)

COLUMN B

a) sleepy and confused
b) sent
c) costs
d) hoped
e) advice
f) group
g) directly
h) slowly
i) friendship
j) watch
k) showed
l) people one is
   responsible for
m) start
n) too fat
o) forgotten
p) punishment
q) gotten too old for

Vocabulary links

Part of our understanding of a text is based on recognition of the links
between words – words that mean the same as each other, that relate to
parts of the same thing, and so on. Answer these questions about
"vocabulary links."

1. In lines 1–15, find another word that means the same as *boy* (line 9).
2. In lines 16–26, find another word for *help* (line 20) and an adjective
   describing people who help.
3. In lines 56–72, find two nouns and a verb having to do with
   involvement (line 56).
4. In lines 56–72, find another word meaning *was upset* (line 63).

Why?

You will probably want to look back at the text, and think about what you have read, to decide on the answers to some of these questions.

1. Why did McClaughlin think the boys started fires?
2. Why did McClaughlin visit a lot of fire stations?
3. Why do firemen talk to the boys about fire prevention?
4. Why do firemen take the boys to ball games?

Inference

Find evidence in the text for the following:

1. Once a boy is labeled an arsonist, he is more likely to commit other crimes.
2. Boys who set fires are sometimes trying to get rid of things that cause problems in their lives.

11 Lions at work and play

This is part of an article about lions' habits by some people who observed them very closely. Read it slowly, more than once if you want. Feel free to stop to think about what you have read.

Lions are opportunists; they prefer to eat without having to do too much work. When resting in the shade, they are also watching the sky, and if they see vultures swooping down, it is off and away. Even in the heat of the day they will suddenly rouse themselves and run a mile across the plains to find out what is going on. If another animal has made a kill, they will drive it off and take the kill for themselves. A grown lion can easily consume 60 pounds of meat at a single feeding. Often they eat until it seems painful for them to lie down.

The lionesses, being leaner and swifter, are better hunters than the males, who look a bit like moving haystacks during the day. The males don't mind; after the kill they move in and take the best share.

Most kills are made at night or just before dawn. In four years at Etosha we have witnessed many, many daylight attempts but only ten kills. We estimate the daytime ratio at around twenty attempts for one kill.

When lions are lying in ambush around a water hole, the atmosphere is electric. They flatten. Their haunches bunch up. They can charge at any second, so we keep ready with our cameras. Meanwhile, the wind is dry and our eyes tire from the sun's glare. Two days in a row we waited at such a water hole with plenty of prey and lions crouching 20 yards away. Yet they didn't make a single charge. It can be very frustrating. But that only adds to the exhilaration we feel when we do get dramatic pictures.

The kill is the exclamation point in the day-to-day existence of the lion, since these great beasts spend most of their time, about 20 hours a day, sleeping and resting.

Lions are social cats, and during these times of leisure they love to rub against each other. After drinking at a water hole, a lioness rests her chin on another's back. When walking past lazing members of their pride, young lions often touch faces with the adults, an act of bonding among members of the group. The gamboling cubs make contact with all.

Do you have the main ideas?

Here are nine sentences. Only six of them express important ideas from the text. The other ideas are in the text, but they are not the author's main concerns. Choose the six main points. Then compare answers with other students before discussing them with your teacher.

1. Lions can wait for a long time for animals to come near enough to kill.
2. Lions watch the sky for vultures.
3. Lions do little but hunt, eat, rest, and sleep.
4. Lions stop about 20 yards from their prey and wait for the prey to come closer.
5. Lionesses are better hunters, but lions eat better.
6. Lions prefer to eat an animal that has died or been killed than to kill one themselves.
7. An adult lion can consume 60 pounds of meat at a time.
8. Lions do not usually kill animals during the day.
9. Lions touch one another a lot.

Guessing words from context

Three things can help you guess words you don't know:
– what you find in the text,
– what you know about similar words, and
– what you know about the world.
Guess the probable meaning of each word or expression in italics.

1. Since vultures are birds, *swooping* (line 5) is probably a way of
    _____.
2. The lionesses are better hunters because they are *leaner and swifter*.
    What would make animals better hunters? What might these words
    mean?
3. *Many daylight attempts but only ten kills* tells you that to *attempt*
    probably means to _____.
4. If *glare* comes from the sun and tires your eyes, it is probably
    _____.

Now try to guess the meanings of these words and expressions:

5. *rouse themselves* (line 7)
6. *kill* (line 10)
7. *consume* (line 11)
8. *lying in ambush* (line 25)
9. *exhilaration* (line 35)

Inference

Find evidence in the text for the following:

1. Lions are stronger than most of the other hunting animals who live in the same place.
2. Lions can see better at night than most of the animals they hunt.
3. Lions hunt in groups.
4. Lions usually make one kill a day.
5. Lions feel themselves part of a group rather than part of a two-parent family.

12 Burnout

Here is an article about a common psychological problem caused by life in the modern world. Read it carefully, stopping to think about what you have read from time to time. Read it more than once if you want.

© 1973 The Register and Tribune Syndicate, Inc.

Schoolteachers and full-time house-wives with children at home are among the highest-risk groups likely to suffer from burnout, says Michael Lauder-dale, director of the University of Texas' School of Social Work's research center, who began studying burnout 10 years ago. He first noticed symptoms of the condition among human service agency workers, but says the condition affects everyone to a degree. Burnout, he believes, comes when "we have expectations of our jobs, careers, marriages, or lives, and the reality we are experiencing is less than our expectations.

"We're in a time of high ambiguity about what life means in terms of social roles and in terms of what we're to do with our lives. I don't think that people have greater expectations now than in the past – I think it's just harder to keep your experiences in place because the times keep changing on you. An example of the rapidly changing times would be a young college student who is advised to get a degree in business. "If you're a sophomore now, by the time you get the degree, people with business degrees could be a glut on the market. The idea that the private sector could solve most of the world's problems could vanish by then."

Lauderdale divides the symptoms of burnout into three stages. First is confusion. The worker may voice general complaints, such as "I don't feel very good" or "I just don't have any pep." Sometimes, chronic backaches, headaches, or colds appear. A worker may seem to lose his sense of humor. He may seem inattentive in a discussion because of the list of things to do running through his mind.

45 Moderate burnout is characterized by more illness and absenteeism, and a "cocoon phenomenon" begins. In that state, workers "seem to have gray faces at 3 p.m. in the office, but after
50 five, it's like a butterfly coming out of a cocoon. Their voices lilt and they are spontaneous when they walk out of the office." The "cocoon phenomenon" is a result of people compartmentalizing
55 their lives, Lauderdale feels. Accompanying that is "lots of clock-watching and counting the days until Friday."

In the third stage of burnout, which he terms despair, "the person pulls into
60 a shell and minimizes work and social contacts as much as possible. There is depression and crying, an increase in drinking, risk-taking and drugs. I related a lot of my work with abusing
65 parents as being the third stage of burnout. They are highly burned out as parents."

Although the bulk of literature about burnout is work-related, the syndrome
70 can occur in any of the multiple roles most people perform – spouse, friend, parent, employee, supervisor. Also, burnout in a job may not begin at work, but may be a spillover from the work-

er's dissatisfaction with other roles, 75 such as being the parent of a teenager.

People can learn to improve their skills at recognizing burnout and at doing something about it, Lauderdale suggests. A frequently used low-risk 80 strategy is one he calls "the quick break." Examples include rearranging the furniture, getting a new haircut or new clothes, taking a vacation, or going to a concert or football game. Other 85 major change responses include compromising and trying to accept the current level of success or income, moving to a new environment or situation, or changing oneself by lowering expec- 90 tations of work or redefining its meaning.

Labeling the syndrome with the buzzword "burnout" tends to trivialize the problem and make it lose its mean- 95 ing, he cautions. "I would emphasize that burnout isn't a passing fad, and it goes way beyond the work world. I don't think men suffer more than women, but I think men may have more burnout on 100 the job, while women get burned out on family life. Work is still a place of wonder and promise for many women new to it."

human service agency workers: people whose job is to help people, for example, social workers, psychologists, and ambulance drivers
ambiguity: uncertainty

buzzword: a colorful, fashionable word that is often overused

---

Summary skills

Write the numbers 1 to 8 on a piece of paper, for the eight paragraphs in the article. Then choose the best title for each paragraph from the list below, and write the title letter next to the paragraph number. Be careful: There are eleven titles in all, but you will need only eight.

a) Despair
b) The quick break
c) Not only at work
d) Physical illness
e) Stage 1
f) Dealing with burnout

g) Lasting and universal
h) College students
i) Stage 2
j) Why does burnout happen?
k) Who suffers from burnout?

Guessing words from context

Find words or phrases in the text that seem to correspond to the definitions given below.

Example (in lines 17–33): people's places in society
Answer: social roles

Now find words or phrases for these meanings in lines 17–33:
1. a second-year student
2. too numerous for the available jobs
3. business that is not government-run

Find words for these meanings in lines 34–44:
4. evidence of a disease
5. energy
6. repeated

Find words for these meanings in lines 58–76:
7. child-beating
8. most

Find words or phrases for these meanings in lines 93–104:
9. make the problem seem unimportant
10. thing that will soon disappear

Making connections

Misunderstandings sometimes happen because we do not realize what is meant by a word like *she* or *it*. Practice making this connection by giving the meaning of each word or phrase in italics.

Example (line 51): *Their* voices lilt...
Answer: Their means the workers.

1. He first noticed symptoms of *the condition*...(line 9)
2. Accompanying *that* is "lots of clock-watching..." (line 56)
3. *They* are highly burned out as parents. (line 66)
4. ...*the syndrome* can occur in any of the multiple roles...(line 69)
5. ...make *it* lose its meaning,...(line 95)
6. "...many women new to *it*." (line 104)

Why?

This exercise asks you to use your own knowledge of the world to think about the facts in the text.

1. What expectations do you think human service agency workers have trouble with?
2. What is special about *five* (line 50)?
3. Why can being the parent of a teenager head to burnout (line 76)?
4. Why is "the quick break" called a *low-risk* strategy (line 80)?

Part 4 Narrative: What happened

13 The diamond

This is part of a short story by Doris Lessing called "Out of the Fountain." Read it carefully, more than once if you want, before doing the exercises.

There was a man called Ephraim who lived in Johannesburg. His father was to do with diamonds, as had been his father. The family were immigrants. This is still true of all people from Johannesburg, a city a century old. Ephraim was a middle son, not brilliant or stupid, not good or bad. He was nothing 5 in particular. His brothers became diamond merchants, but Ephraim was not cut out for anything immediately obvious, and so at last he was apprenticed to an uncle to learn the trade of diamond-cutting.

To cut a diamond perfectly is an act like a samurai's sword- 10 thrust, or a master archer's centered arrow. When an important diamond is shaped a man may spend a week, or even weeks, studying it, accumulating powers of attention, memory, in- tuition, till he has reached that moment when he finally knows that a tap, no more, at just *that* point of tension in the stone 15 will split it exactly *so*.

While Ephraim learned to do this, he lived at home in a Johannesburg suburb; and his brothers and sisters married and had families. He was the son who took his time about getting

married, and about whom the family first joked, saying that   20
he was choosy; and then they remained silent when others
talked of him with that edge on their voices, irritated, a little
malicious, even frightened, which is caused by those men and
women who refuse to fulfill the ordinary purposes of nature.
The kind ones said he was a good son, working nicely under   25
his uncle Ben, and living respectably at home, and on Sunday
nights playing poker with bachelor friends. He was twenty-
five, then thirty, thirty-five, forty. His parents became old and
died, and he lived alone in the family house. People stopped
noticing him. Nothing was expected of him.   30

Then a senior person became ill, and Ephraim was asked to
fly in his stead to Alexandria for a special job. A certain rich
merchant of Alexandria had purchased an uncut diamond as a
present for his daughter, who was to be married shortly. He
wished only the best for the diamond. Ephraim, revealed by   35
this happening as one of the world's master diamond-cutters,
flew to Egypt, spent some days in communion with the stone
in a quiet room in the merchant's house, and then caused it
to fall apart into three lovely pieces. These were for a ring and
earrings.   40

Now he should have flown home again; but the merchant
asked him to dinner. An odd chance that – unusual. Not many
people got inside that rich closed world. But perhaps the merchant had become infected by the week of rising tension while
Ephraim became one with the diamond in a quiet room.   45

At dinner Ephraim met the girl for whom the jewels were
destined.

Johannesburg: the largest city in South Africa
thrust: a sudden, forceful push

Summary skills

Write the numbers 1 to 6 on a piece of paper, for the six paragraphs in
the story. Then choose the best title for each paragraph from the list,
and write the title letter next to the paragraph number. Be careful:
There are ten titles in all, but you will need only six.

a) The art of diamond cutting

b) The girl

c) Rising tension

d) Invitation to dinner

e) Ephraim becomes a diamond
   cutter

f) A time-consuming job

g) A city of immigrants

h) Ephraim's family

i) An unexpected job

j) Single and middle-aged

Making connections

Misunderstandings sometimes happen because we do not realize what is meant by a word like *she* or *it*. This exercise will give you practice in making the connections between these words and their meanings. Give the meaning of each word in italics. (The meaning can be in the same sentence or elsewhere in the text.)

Example (in line 5): *He* was nothing in particular.
Answer: He means *Ephraim.*

1. His father was to do with diamonds, as had been *his father.* (line 2)
2. While Ephraim learned to do *this*, he lived at home in a Johannesburg suburb; ... (line 17)
3. Then a senior person became ill, and Ephraim was asked to fly in *his* stead to Alexandria for a special job. (line 32)
4. Ephraim, revealed by this happening as one of the world's master diamond-cutters, flew to Egypt, spent some days in communion with the stone in a quiet room in the merchant's house, and then caused *it* to fall apart into three lovely pieces. (line 38)

Inference

It is important to understand what a text says, and what it suggests. It is also important *not* to think a story says or suggests more than it does. Try to do this exercise without looking back at the text; but do read the text again if the exercise begins to seem too difficult. Just answer yes or no to each question.

Does the text say:
1. how many brothers Ephraim had?
2. what Ephraim's brothers did?
3. who Ephraim worked for?
4. how long Ephraim was an apprentice before cutting his first diamond?
5. whether Ephraim had any nephews or nieces?
6. where Ephraim was living when he was sent to Egypt?
7. whether Ephraim's friends thought he would become famous?
8. how many children the rich merchant had?
9. where Ephraim was when he cut the diamond?
10. whether Ephraim met the girl before cutting the diamond?

Opinions and feelings

In this story, the author communicates opinions and feelings – her own and her characters' – by telling the reader what the characters did. This exercise will help you think about those ideas and feelings. Match each phrase in column A with its best description in column B. There are some extra descriptions in column B.

COLUMN A

1. Ephraim as a child
2. A professional diamond cutter
3. How Ephraim's not getting married made some people feel
4. Ephraim's private life in Johannesburg
5. Ephraim's ability to cut diamonds
6. Ephraim's approach to cutting the rich merchant's diamond
7. The rich merchant, observing Ephraim's way of working

COLUMN B

a) difficult
b) impressed
c) uninteresting
d) unexceptional
e) mystical
f) highly skilled
g) exceptional
h) bored
i) violent
j) uncomfortable

14   A gentleman thief

Here is an article about an unusual thief. After every paragraph you will find a short summary of what you have just read. But the summary has mistakes in it! Put a line through the mistaken words or phrases in the summary and write the correct ones; or, on a separate piece of paper, write down the mistakes and corrections.

Example: This is an article about a ~~doctor~~. *thief*

At 33, Josef Streit was every inch the impeccable young West German businessman. A handsome man, he drove from job to job in a silver-gray Porsche. Between 1970 and 1979, aided by his brother Stefan and two friends, he took in a comfortable but hardly greedy income of about $330,000 – or so the authorities estimate. As it happened, Streit and his collaborators accumulated this income from the safes of 28 banks in Austria.   5

                                                                                                                    10

Summary 1

Between 1970 and 1979 a middle-aged businessman named Josef Streit, with two other men, drove a Volkswagen from one bank to another. They stole enormous amounts of money from 28 Austrian banks.

Streit was a deft safecracker who never used force – either against people or safes. "He has never shot, strangled or threatened," wrote Austrian Columnist Richard Nimmerrichter in a sympathetic portrait in Vienna's daily *Neue Kronenzeitung*. "He was an undisputed artist of his trade." According to Streit's own testimony, it took him only 19 minutes to open the toughest safe he ever encountered. His only sin beyond larceny seemed to be a touch of arrogance. On his last job, early in 1979, he left the safe door   15

                                                                                                                    20

---

trade: job
larceny: theft

open and a million Austrian schillings ($80,000) behind. With the money was a note: "We don't need all that much."

Summary 2

Streit never hurt anyone, but he damaged the safes he opened. He was an artist in his spare time. When he opened a safe, he did it slowly and carefully, and he left the safe door open after every job.

That caper was Streit's undoing. A witness spotted an accomplice's car and, last March, Streit was arrested, subsequently tried, and sent to Austria's Stein Prison to serve a six-year sentence. He boasted at his trial that he would continue breaking the law: "I am a thief and I shall use every opportunity." Despite the warning, prison officials last June blithely moved Streit from the jail's cobblery to its blacksmith shop. One day during the week before Christmas, Streit disappeared after a 3 p.m. roll call. Searchers found all cells and doors securely locked. Streit, it seemed, had managed to make a set of master keys and let himself out.

Summary 3

Streit was caught because someone saw his car; he was sent to prison, and he promised to stop breaking the law. In prison, he managed to steal some keys and get out. He left all the prison doors open.

Not to freedom, though. After crossing into Bavaria, Streit purposely aroused the suspicion of West German customs police, got himself identified and arrested. "I want to improve my lot," he explained to the surprised cops. "As a German citizen I cannot be extradited to Austria. German courts pass much milder sentences for crimes like mine and will deduct the time I served in Stein Prison. I may be free in a few months."

cobblery: place where shoes are made
blacksmith shop: place where iron is worked

Summary 4

Streit crossed into Bavaria and tried not to get arrested. This was because he preferred to be sentenced by an Austrian court.

Temporarily jailed in Bavaria's Landshut Prison, Streit persuaded his keepers to let him make a Christmas Eve telephone call to his former warden, Karl Schreiner of Stein Prison. "I'm sorry if I caused trouble," Schreiner quoted the thief. "I didn't want to embarrass anybody by escaping. Conditions weren't that bad. In fact the food was better than it is here." Streit reassured the Austrian warden that he had made his escape from Stein Prison without any help from his jailers, adding, "Don't worry about others escaping. Only a burglar of my outstanding ability can do it."   50   55   60

Summary 5

Streit phoned his Austrian warden to say "thank you." He said it was easy for prisoners to escape from the Austrian jail.

Last week West German authorities were still pondering what to do with Streit. Though he cannot be extradited, he can be retried in West Germany for the crimes committed in Austria: double jeopardy does not apply. In West Germany, sentences for burglary range from three months to ten years, and while Streit might expect leniency for his nonviolent ways, the number of his crimes and his escape might incline a court toward harsher punishment. If Streit is retried and draws a stiff sentence, he could always try for a job in the blacksmith shop.   65   70

double jeopardy: the rule that a person cannot be judged twice for the same crime

Summary 6

Stein cannot be tried by a German court. It is certain he will spend a long time in German prison.

Guessing words from context

Find words or expressions in the text that seem to correspond to the definitions given below.

Example (in lines 25–38): a check to see if people are present
Answer: roll call

Now find words for these meanings in lines 1–24:
1. people who help someone do a job
2. expert
3. most difficult

Find words for these meanings in lines 25–38:
4. criminal job
5. then
6. without worrying

Find words for these meanings in lines 39–61:
7. policemen (slang)
8. director of a prison
9. exceptional

Find words for these meanings in lines 62–73:
10. thinking about
11. long

Making connections

Give the meanings of the words and phrases in italics.

Example: ... Streit and *his collaborators* ... (lines 8–9)
Answer: *His collaborators* means his brother Stefan and two friends.

1. ... Streit and his collaborators accumulated *this income* ... (line 9)
2. "He was an undisputed artist of *his trade*." (line 17)
3. With *the money* was a note ... (line 23)
4. "*We* don't need all that much." (line 23)
5. *That caper* was Streit's undoing. (line 25)
6. "In fact the food was better than it is *here*." (line 56)
7. "Only a burglar of my outstanding ability can *do it*." (line 61)

Facts and figures

Find information in the text to help you calculate the answers to these questions.

1. What was the average amount Streit stole from each bank?
2. How many schillings are there to a dollar?
3. How long did Streit spend in Stein Prison?
4. If Stein had to go back to an Austrian prison, how much time would he have to spend there?
5. How old was Streit when he began stealing from Austrian banks?
6. Where did Streit spend Christmas?

15 Great operatic disasters

These are the first two stories from a book about technical disasters during opera performances. Read them carefully, more than once if you want, before doing the exercises.

Tosca: *City Center, New York, 1960*

This catastrophe is due, not to misunderstanding and incompetence, but entirely to ill-will between the stage staff and the soprano. With diabolical cunning they permitted her, after several stormy rehearsals, to complete her first performance without mishap until the very last moment, when Tosca throws herself off the battlements of the Castel Sant'Angelo. What normally happens is that on her cry "*Scarpia, davanti a Dio*" she hurls herself off and lands on a mattress four feet below. This large young American singer landed not on a mattress, but – perish the thought – on a *trampoline.* It is said that she came up fifteen times before the curtain fell – sometimes upside down, then the right way up – now laughing in delirious glee, now screaming with rage. ...Worse still, it seems that the unhappy lady was unable to reappear in New York because the Center's faithful audience, remembering the trampoline, would have burst into laughter. She had to remove herself to San Francisco, where of course no such grotesque incident could possibly occur....

Tosca: *San Francisco Opera, 1961*

One must remember that *Tosca* is thought to be an "easy" opera for a producer; there are in effect only three principals – Tosca, Cavaradossi and Scarpia. The other participants amount only to the first-act chorus (some rehearsal needed here), the second-act choir (off stage thank God) and the third-act execution squad (no problem, they don't sing . . .). Alas, it is thus that fatal errors happen. On this particular occasion that firing squad was composed of enthusiastic local college boys, totally ignorant of the story. As the dress rehearsal had to be canceled because of illness, the execution squad appeared on the opening night only five minutes after their first and only consultation with the producer. In a hurry, he had told them, "O.K., boys. When the stage-manager cues you, slow-march in, wait until the officer lowers his sword, then shoot." "But how do we get off?" "Oh – well, exit with the principals." (This is the standard American instruction for minor characters, servants, etc.)

The audience, therefore, saw the following: a group of soldiers marched on to the stage but stopped dead in its tracks at the sight of *two* people, not one as they had assumed – a man and a woman, both looking extremely alarmed. They pointed their hesitant rifles at the man, but he started giving strange glances at the woman . . . they pointed them at her, but she made a series of violently negative gestures – but then what else would she do if she was about to be shot? The opera was called Tosca, it was evidently tragic, the enormous woman on stage was presumably Tosca herself, the officer was raising his sword. . . .

Thus it happened. *They shot Tosca instead of Cavaradossi.* To their amazement they then saw the man, some twenty yards away, fall lifeless to the ground, while the person they *had* shot rushed over to him. What could they do? They had shot one of the principals – though admittedly the wrong one – and their next instruction was "Exit with the principals." Spoletta and his minions burst on to the stage and Tosca – could it be true? – took up her position on top of the battlements. She jumped, and there was only one thing to do – as the curtain slowly descended the whole firing-squad threw themselves after her. . . .

stage: the place in a theater (usually at the front) where the actors perform
trampoline:

principals: most important actors
execution squad: a group of soldiers who shoot a criminal condemned to death (firing-squad)
dress rehearsal: the last practice performance of an opera, with all the actors present in their costumes

---

Summary skills 1

Here is a summary of the first story. Fill in the blanks with appropriate words.

In New York in 1960, the _____ in *Tosca* was

not very friendly with the _____ workers. So instead of

giving her a _____ to fall on when she _____

from the castle in the last act, they gave her a _____.

Instead of disappearing, she _____ up behind the

battlements again and again. She had to _____ New York as a

result of this incident.

Summary skills 2

Here are some pictures illustrating the San Francisco disaster, but they are not in order. Your task is to find the correct order.

Guessing words from context

Match each word in italics in column A with the meaning in column B
that comes closest to it. Column B has some extra meanings.

COLUMN A
1. This catastrophe is due...entirely to *ill-will*
   between the stage staff and the soprano. (line 4)
2. ...after several *stormy* rehearsals,...(line 6)
3. ...to complete her first performance without
   mishap...(line 8)
4. ...she *hurls* herself off and lands on a mattress...
   (line 12)
5. ...now laughing in delirious *glee*,...(line 19)
6. ...a group of soldiers marched on to the stage but
   stopped *dead in its tracks*...(line 54)
7. ...she made a series of violently negative *gestures*
   ...(line 61)

COLUMN B
a) pretending to be shot
b) joy
c) in bad weather
d) hand movements
e) marches
f) full of disagreement
g) bad planning
h) throws
i) suddenly and completely
j) something going wrong
k) bad feelings

Reading carefully for details

Mark each sentence with **T** if it is true according to the text and **F** if it
is false according to the text. You will probably have to look back at
the text, and think about what you have read, to decide on some of the
answers.

1. People often go to see more than one opera each year at the City
   Center in New York.
2. In both of the performances described, Tosca was played by a fat
   woman.
3. The author of the text is sure that Tosca bounced exactly 15 times in
   the New York performance.
4. *Tosca* is an easy opera for a producer, according to the author of the
   text.
5. The first-act chorus in *Tosca* sings on stage.
6. The boys in the firing squad liked opera very much.
7. The disaster in San Francisco was the fault of the execution squad.

16 Poison

Here is a newspaper article about a dangerous chemical. Read it carefully, more than once if you want, but do not worry if you cannot understand every word. Feel free to stop while you are reading to think back over what you have read.

WASHINGTON (AP) – For three years, doctors couldn't figure out why horses died and people got sick at an eastern Missouri riding stable. In frustration, they decided to try one last test, looking for traces of the deadly but little-known chemical dioxin.

At a Centers for Disease Control (CDC) laboratory in Chamblee, Ga., researchers prepared a weak solution of the stable's soil and swabbed it on the ears of rabbits.

Within the week, they were dead. That was in 1974, and the horror of dioxin in Missouri was just beginning to emerge.

Today the problem is still unsolved, and what has happened in the long years in between is a story of human suffering.

"I'm positive this dioxin ruined my health," says Judy Piatt, the former owner of the tainted stable whose two daughters still suffer from the chemical. "Every time you think things are getting better, one of the kids has an incident where their hair falls out, they get nosebleeds and fatigue.

"There's something about this chemical that's just evil."

Last week, the federal government took one step to deal with Missouri's dioxin menace. It promised $33 million to buy out the St. Louis suburb of Times Beach so its 2,400 residents can restart their lives elsewhere.

But Times Beach is only the beginning in Missouri. Twenty-one other sites are tainted with dioxin, from a wastewater treatment plant in Neosho to a churchyard in St. Louis to the horse stable Piatt once owned near Moscow Mills.

ALMOST CERTAINLY, there are other sites yet undiscovered; more than 42 pounds of the potent poison has not been traced.

In 1971 – when the first dioxin-contaminated waste was sprayed on Piatt's riding arena to keep down dust – few health researchers knew dioxin existed.

Even now, knowledge about the toxin is incomplete. Scientists argue about alleged links to cancer, nerve and liver damage, and birth defects.

The poisoning of Missouri started at a plant in Verona, in the southwest corner of the state. The plant made the skin cleanser hexachlorophene using a process that left an oily black residue containing dioxin.

At first, the company – Northeast Pharmaceutical and Chemical Co. – sent its waste to Louisiana for incineration. Later, because of cash problems, the company sold the residue to a local waste-oil dealer, Russell Bliss of St. Louis.

NORTHEAST, NOW defunct, claimed it told Bliss of the waste's dangers. Bliss steadfastly denies that.

What is certain is that he resold the companies' waste oil – at a profit – for re-refining or to keep down dust, as on the roads of Times Beach.

He sprayed the riding arena at Piatt's Shenandoah Stables in 1971 with "oil" that was really undiluted residue from Northeast, contaminated with levels of dioxin 30,000 times greater than the Environmental Protection Agency (EPA) has deemed a health hazard.

People at the arena noticed a stench and some got sick. Within days, hundreds of sparrows were found dead on the ground. In all, about 75 horses became ill and died at Shenandoah and two other arenas sprayed with the oil.

FRIGHTENED, PIATT became an am-
80 ateur detective, trailing Bliss' trucks, photographing them as they picked up and
dumped wastes.

In late 1972, Piatt says she took her find-
ings to the EPA and the state Division of
85 Health – including a list of 18 sites where
she saw Bliss trucks dump waste. The list
included Times Beach ("This should be
looked into closely . . . ," she wrote).

The menace could have been uncovered
90 as early as 1972, when researchers overlooked a test result that showed the dioxin
taint in the stable's dirt, says CDC expert
Renate Kimbrough.

In 1974, the CDC rabbits died and dioxin
95 was identified. State investigators traced the
chemical through Bliss' trucking firm to the
Verona plant.

The pace picked up once again in October
1979, when a former Northeast Pharmaceutical employee tipped the EPA to a secret 100
dioxin dump at a Missouri farm.

By 1980, the EPA came back to Piatt and
asked her to lay out once again the routes
of Bliss' trucks nearly a decade earlier. The
list of possible dioxin sites in the state grew 105
to more than 100.

Today, it is all far from over.

Tainted sites remain untouched. Questions are being raised about other sites and
other chemicals. The final bill has yet to be 110
tallied for the poisoning of Missouri.

horror: frightening reality
alleged: said to be true
plant: factory

incineration: burning
stench: bad smell
tallied: added up

Summary skills

Here is a chart of the main events in the article, in the order in which they
happened. (Like many articles and stories, this article does not tell the
events in the exact order they happened.) On a separate sheet of paper,
write descriptions for illustrations 3, 4, 5, 7, 9, and 12.

1. Northeast made
skin cleanser
leaving dioxin.

2. Burning dioxin was
too expensive.

3.

4. (1971)

5.

6. Piatt followed
Bliss' trucks.

7. (1972)

8. CDC overlooked
test result (1972).

9. (1974)

10. Piatt helped
EPA find other sites.

11. Times Beach people
were paid to move.

12. (now)

Guessing words from context

Match each word in italics in column A with the meaning in column B that comes closest to it. Column B has some extra meanings.

COLUMN A
1. ... and *swabbed* it on the ears of rabbits. (line 10)
2. ... was just beginning to *emerge*. (line 13)
3. "I'm *positive* this dioxin ruined my health." (line 17)
4. Twenty-one other *sites* are tainted with dioxin ... (line 32)
5. Northeast ... *claimed* it told Bliss of the waste's dangers. (line 59)
6. ... Piatt became an *amateur* detective ... (lines 79–80)
7. The *menace* could have been uncovered ... (line 89)
8. ... researchers *overlooked* a test result ... (lines 90–91)
9. *Tainted* sites remain untouched. (line 108)

COLUMN B
a) places
b) danger
c) plants
d) put
e) said
f) be forgotten
g) become known
h) didn't notice (but should have)
i) clean
j) full-time
k) sure
l) not professional
m) poisoned

Making connections

Misunderstandings sometimes happen because we do not make the connection between a word like *it* and its meaning earlier in the text. Practice making these connections by giving the meaning of each word in italics.

Example: ... and swabbed *it* on the ears of rabbits. (line 10)
Answer: It means *a weak solution of the stable's soil.*

1. Within the week, *they* were dead. (line 11)
2. *It* promised $33 million ... (line 28)
3. ... so *its* 2,400 residents can restart their lives elsewhere. (line 29)
4. ... sent *its* waste to Louisiana ... (line 54)
5. ... photographing *them* as they picked up and dumped wastes. (line 81)
6. ... ("This should be looked into closely, ..." *she* wrote). (line 88)

Reading carefully for details

You may want to look back at the text while answering these questions. Write **T** if the sentence is true according to the text, **F** if the sentence is false according to the text, and **DS** if the text doesn't say.

1. Dioxin killed rabbits when it was sprayed at Piatt's stables.
2. All of the places where dioxin was put have now been found.
3. Bliss knew that dioxin was dangerous.
4. Only animals were affected by the dioxin at Shenandoah Stables.
5. Northeast Pharmaceutical hid some dioxin.
6. It took the Environmental Protection Agency eight years to pay full attention to Piatt.

Part 5 Persuasion: Why you should do it

17 The family room

The advertisement on the opposite page is by a company that makes and sells fairly expensive, traditional furniture. Read it, more than once if you want, and pause as often as you like.

Summary skills

Write the numbers 1 to 5 on a piece of paper, for the five paragraphs in the advertisement. Then choose the best title for each paragraph from the list below, and write the title letter next to the paragraph number. Be careful: There are seven titles in all, but you will need only five.

a) Home, not school
b) Family traditions
c) Modern problems
d) A place to be together

e) Crime today
f) Learning to live
g) Beauty not enough

Guessing words from context

1. What area does the word *drama* (line 9) come from – business, agriculture, theater . . . ?
2. Is *erosion* (line 15) good or bad?
3. Complete this sentence: *Juvenile delinquency* (line 19) is one of the . . .
4. Is a *trauma* (line 20) good or bad?
5. Guess the meaning of *over-burdened* (line 22).

Inference

1. Put a √ after the statements that are implied by the opinions expressed in the advertisement and an X after those that are not.
   a) Children of single parents will probably be unhappy adults.
   b) Teenage children should be encouraged to develop their own interests even if this means going out every evening.
   c) Children begin taking drugs because they are not taught properly at home.
   d) One way of improving society is by more government spending on social projects.
2. Do you think this advertisement will sell furniture? How and why? Discuss your answers with another student.

The family is more important than the family room.

It doesn't matter which room a family chooses to gather in. It could be a favorite corner of the kitchen, or a wood panelled den. What does matter is that they choose
5 to be together. For it is the support, the strength, the bonds and traditions of the family that give us what we all need most in life. A good home.

Home is the stage where the drama
10 of life is played. It's the classroom where children learn right from wrong. Where old-fashioned ideals like courage and honesty, respect for oneself and others are passed down from one generation to the next.

15 We are concerned about the erosion of these values that should be taught at home. We see the growing problems of society—broken homes, crime, drugs, and juvenile delinquency—and are shocked
20 by the trauma they inflict on families, especially children.

Our over-burdened schools can no longer solve these problems confronting our society. There is only one place where
25 we can regain the values and integrity that will cure these ills. We must turn to the home—our piece of the world—the place where it all begins.

For fifty years, Ethan Allen has been
30 dedicated to helping Americans create beautiful environments for their homes. But we know it takes more than fine quality furnishings to make a good home. It takes the love, respect and understanding of
35 those who share it together.

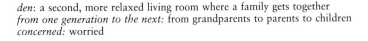

Ethan Allen Galleries
A Good Home Lasts a Lifetime.

© 1982 Ethan Allen Inc. An INTERCO

den: a second, more relaxed living room where a family gets together
from one generation to the next: from grandparents to parents to children
concerned: worried

18 Better left unsaid

Here is an opinion column from a magazine about how honest people should be with their families and friends. Read it carefully, more than once if you want, but do not worry if there are words you do not understand as long as you get the general meaning.

During the past ten or fifteen years a great deal of attention has been given to "telling it like it is," or "letting it all hang out." My impression is that
5 this overzealous devotion to speaking one's mind has more often led to hurt feelings and ruined relationships than to great joy and fulfillment.

I think we generally agree that *never*
10 expressing real feelings and repressing all less-than-lovely thoughts about each other hardly leads to constructive communication. It's a great relief to allow ourselves the luxury of
15 acknowledging our human frailties and pursuing more honest relationships with others. But we need to strike a balance between telling it all and telling nothing.
20 Recently I received a letter from a mother who had been persuaded by her troubled twenty-five-year-old son to attend a weekend marathon with him. Under pressure from the group, her defenses collapsed and she heard 25 herself telling her son for the first time that he had been an accident – that she hadn't been planning to have a child. He in turn told her that he couldn't recall a single day in his 30 childhood that he'd been happy.

"At that time," this woman wrote, "it seemed helpful. We cried and we made up; I thought telling the truth had been good for us. But the trouble 35 is, it wasn't the whole truth. By the time Tommy was born I *did* want him, and at times he *was* happy. Ever since that day, we've both been haunted by some terrible feelings we shared." 40

I must admit I've come to the conclusion that some things are better left unsaid. Honesty is a fine policy as long as we know what the truth really is – but most of the time we don't. 45 It's a fine goal to encourage children to express their real feelings. And many marriages have been saved by an open confrontation of deep and painful misunderstandings. But we 50 need a new sense of balance. Disclosure is not a panacea for every problem nor even an end in itself. It's useful

---

letting it all hang out: saying exactly how you feel
devotion to: belief in   *frailties:* weaknesses
marathon: non-stop meeting where people try to solve their psychological problems by talking
   in a group (an unusual meaning of this word)
made up: became friends again
disclosure: telling something that has been a secret

and freeing under some circum-
55 stances and terribly hurtful and dam-
aging under others.

It's a good idea, I think, to bite your
tongue for ten or fifteen minutes before saying what's on your mind. Try
to decide whether it's going to open 60
up new and better avenues of communication or leave wounds that may
never heal.

Do you have the main ideas?

Here are six sentences. Only four of them express important ideas from the
text. The other ideas are in the text, but they are not the author's main
concerns. Choose the four main points, and compare answers with some
other students before discussing them with your teacher.

1. What seems to be the whole truth may in fact be only part of it.
2. It is a relief to admit our weaknesses.
3. It is sometimes good to say exactly what's on your mind.
4. You should think carefully before "telling it like it is."
5. Sometimes it can hurt more than help to say what you think or feel.
6. It is good to encourage children to express their real feelings.

Guessing words from context

Match each word or expression in italics in column A with the meaning in
column B that comes closest to it. Column B has some extra meanings.

COLUMN A
1. ... this *overzealous* devotion to speaking one's mind
   ... (line 5)
2. ... the luxury of *acknowledging* our human frailties
   ... (line 15)
3. ... we've both been *haunted* by some terrible
   feelings ... (line 39)
4. Honesty is a fine *policy* ... (line 43)
5. And many marriages have been saved by an open
   confrontation of deep and painful
   misunderstandings. (line 49)
6. Disclosure is not a *panacea* for every problem ...
   (line 52)
7. It's a good idea, I think, to *bite your tongue* for ten or
   fifteen minutes ... (lines 57–58)
8. ... or leave *wounds* that may never heal. (line 62)

COLUMN B
a) discussion
b) hurt places
c) helped
d) too enthusiastic
e) way of acting
f) weak
g) words
h) solution
i) hurt yourself
j) avoid speaking
k) worried
l) thinking about
m) talking openly about

19 Save the children

Here is a magazine advertisement. Read it carefully, more than once if you want. Feel free to stop to think about what you have read.

Save The Children Federation® 48 Wilton Road, Westport, Connecticut 06880

PLEASE READ MY URGENT PLEA
TO HELP SAVE MARIA PASTORA
AND THE OTHER CHILDREN OF HER VILLAGE

Dear Reader:

Imagine an 11-year-old child whose days are often spent scrubbing clothes,   5
raising a baby brother, struggling with heavy farm chores.
Imagine a little girl who knows there will not be enough food for dinner. Who
can't fill her stomach with water because it's contaminated. Who has watched her
life slip away from her father and little brother and sister because the family
could not afford a doctor.   10
Hard to believe? For Maria Pastora, these are the facts of life.
Maria would gladly walk miles to school, but her mother, now alone, needs her
badly at home. Chances are Maria will grow up illiterate. Her future? In many
ways, disastrous.
But for just 52 pennies a day, you can sponsor a child like Maria. Show her   15
that somewhere, someone cares about her plight. Through Save the Children, you
can help Maria's mother get the tools and guidance she needs to turn their meager
half-acre into a source of good food; earn the money she needs to buy clothing
and school supplies for Maria.
To help Maria most, your money is combined with that of other sponsors, so   20
hard-working people can help themselves. Build a school...a health facility...
reclaim land...bring in clean water. This is what Save the Children has been
about since 1932.
For you there are many rewards. The chance to correspond with your sponsored
child. Receive photographs, progress reports. Know you are reaching out to   25
another human being. Not with a handout, but a hand up. That's how Save the
Children works. But without you, it can't work. Please take a moment now to fill
out and mail the coupon below to help a child like Maria and her village.
It can make such a difference...in her life and yours.

For the children,   30

David L. Guyer
President

Not with a handout, but a hand up: not just by giving money, but by helping people to become independent

Summary skills

Choose one subject from the following list and read the text again, making notes about the subject you have chosen. Your notes do not have to be in complete sentences.

   When you have finished the notes, find one or two other people in the class who have chosen the same subject as you. Compare your notes and write a new set of notes that you agree on.

Subjects:
1. School
2. Maria's mother
3. Food and water
4. Sponsoring a child
5. Maria's family life

Guessing words from context

Match each word in italics in column A with the meaning in column B that comes closest to it. Column B has some extra meanings.

COLUMN A
1. Imagine an 11-year-old child whose days are often spent *scrubbing* clothes . . . (line 5)
2. . . . raising a baby brother, *struggling with* heavy farm chores. (line 6)
3. . . . raising a baby brother, struggling with heavy farm *chores*. (line 6)
4. Who can't fill her stomach with water because it's *contaminated*. (line 8)
5. Chances are Maria will grow up *illiterate*. (line 13)
6. Show her that somewhere, someone cares about her *plight*. (line 16)
7. . . . you can help Maria's mother get the tools and guidance she needs to turn their *meager* half-acre into a source of good food; . . . (line 17)
8. To help Maria most, your money is combined with that of other *sponsors*, . . . (line 20)

COLUMN B
a) serious problem
b) in bad health
c) washing
d) jobs
e) buying
f) having great difficulty with
g) small
h) machines
i) people who provide money
j) dirty
k) organizations
l) not able to read or write

Why and how?

This exercise will give you practice in finding connections between different parts of a text. Answer each question in a few words; do not bother to write complete sentences.

1. Find three reasons why Maria is in danger of falling ill.
2. Find the reason Maria's mother is alone.
3. Find three things that could help Maria go to school.
4. Find two things that could keep Maria healthier.
5. Find three ways in which a sponsor communicates with a child.

20 Two letters

The letters on the opposite page were received by a man who owed money to a doctor. The doctor had treated the man's daughter.

Do you have the main ideas?

Perhaps you can do this exercise without looking back at the letters. If not, the questions will help you to find the main ideas. Mark **T** if the sentence is true according to the letters and **F** if it is false according to the letters.

1. The March 5 letter was the first one from Dr. Brown's office about the money the man owed.
2. The March 5 letter is more polite than the March 17 letter.
3. Ms. Marques thinks that $325.00 is a small payment.
4. The March 17 letter contains a threat.
5. In two weeks Ms. Marques will write the same man another letter.

Guessing words from context

Find words or phrases in the two letters that have roughly the meanings given below.

1. record of a patient's bills
2. be polite, and answer
3. pay no attention to
4. enough
5. other choice
6. company that specializes in getting money from people who owe it

Inference

Find evidence in the two letters for the following:

1. Several people work for Dr. Brown.
2. Studies have shown that most people prefer to pay large debts in several installments.
3. If the man telephoned the doctor's office and explained that he was on strike and had no money, they would probably be understanding.
4. Businesses in the United States share information about the way people pay their debts.

G. R. BROWN, M.D.
4231 ████████, ██████, Texas 77002

March 5, 1986

Mr. George ██████
3124 ████████████████
█████████, Texas 77002

Re: $325.00   Account No. ████

Dear Mr. ████████:

    Two weeks ago we wrote to you asking you
to contact us about the above account; as yet
we have not heard from you.
    At the time your daughter needed medical
attention she was treated immediately. We feel
that you should at least extend the courtesy
of replying to our several requests for payment
by making full or partial payments, beginning
now. Even small payments will be accepted if
they are regular ones.
    We expect to hear from you within the next
two weeks, please.

Very truly yours,

Helen Marques

Helen Marques
Office Manager

G. R. BROWN, M.D.
4231 ████████, ██████, Texas 77002

March 17, 1986

Mr. George ██████
3124 ████████████
████████, Texas 77002

Re: $325.00   Account No. ████

Dear Mr. ██████:

    We cannot understand why you continue
to ignore the requests for payment we have
been mailing you. We feel that you have had
ample time to send payment, call, or write
regarding this account.
    If we have not heard from you within two
weeks, we shall have no alternative but to
turn this account over to a collection agency
for payment. Surely you do not want to have
this on your credit record.
    We expect prompt attention to this matter.

Very truly yours,

Helen Marques

Helen Marques
Office Manager

M.D.: Medical Doctor

Part 6 Categories: How things are classified

21 Men and women: Some differences

Here is part of an article on the differences between men and women. Read it carefully, more than once if you want.

Men cannot manufacture blood as efficiently as women can. This makes surgery riskier for men. Men also need more oxygen because they do not breathe as often as women. But men breathe more deeply and this exposes them to another risk. When the air is polluted, they draw more of it into their lungs.　　5

A more recent – and chilling – finding is the effect of automobile and truck exhaust fumes on children's intelligence. These exhaust fumes are the greatest source of lead pollution in cities. Researchers have found that the children　10 with the highest concentration of lead in their bodies have the lowest scores on intelligence tests and that boys score lower than girls. It is possible that these low scores are connected to the deeper breathing that is typical of the male.　　15

Men's bones are larger than women's and they are arranged somewhat differently. The feminine walk that evokes so many whistles is a matter of bone structure. Men have broader shoulders and a narrower pelvis, which enables them to stride out with no waste motion. A woman's wider　20 pelvis, designed for childbearing, forces her to put more movement into each step she takes with the result that she displays a bit of a jiggle and sway as she walks.

If you think a man is brave because he climbs a ladder to clean out the roof gutters, don't forget that it is easier　25 for him than for a woman. The angle at which a woman's thigh is joined to her knees makes climbing awkward for her, no matter whether it is a ladder or stairs or a mountain that she is tackling.

A man's skin is thicker than a woman's and not nearly　30 as soft. The thickness prevents the sun's radiation from getting through, which is why men wrinkle less than women do.

Women have a thin layer of fat just under the skin and there is a plus to this greater fat reserve. It acts as an　35 invisible fur coat to keep a woman warmer in the winter.

Women also stay cooler in summer. The fat layer helps insulate them against heat.

Men's fat is distributed differently. And they do not have　40 that layer of it underneath their skin. In fact, they have considerably less fat than women and more lean mass. Forty-one percent of a man's body is muscle compared to thirty-five percent for women, which means that men have more muscle power. When it comes to strength, almost 90 percent of a man's weight is strength compared to about 50 percent of a woman's weight.

The higher proportion of muscle to fat makes it easier for men to lose weight. Muscle burns up five more calories a pound than fat does just to maintain itself. So when a man goes on a diet, the pounds roll off much faster.

For all men's muscularity they do not have the energy reserves women do. They have more start-up energy, but the fat tucked away in women's nooks and crannies provides a rich energy reserve that men lack.

Cardiologists at the University of Alabama who tested healthy women on treadmills discovered that over the years the female capacity for exercise far exceeds the male capacity. A woman of sixty who is in good health can exercise up to 90 percent of what she could do when she was twenty. A man of sixty has only 60 percent left of his capacity as a twenty-year-old.

surgery: cutting a person open to take out or repair a part of the body that is inside
exhaust fumes: the gases made when an engine runs on gasoline
lead: a heavy metal (Pb), dangerous for humans when eaten or breathed
pelvis: hip bones

Summary skills

Complete the table, using a few words to describe each difference.

	Men	Women
Blood manufacture	less efficient	more efficient
Breathing		
Lead in bodies		
Bones		
Shoulders		
Pelvis		
Climbing		
Skin		
Fat – amount?		
Fat – where?		
Percentage of muscle		
Strength – percentage of weight		
Energy reserves		
Capacity for exercise with aging		

Guessing words from context

Match each word or expression in italics in column A with the meaning in column B that comes closest to it. Column B has some extra meanings.

COLUMN A

1. . . . they draw more of it into their *lungs*. (line 6)
2. A more recent – and *chilling* – finding . . . (line 7)
3. . . . which enables them to *stride out* with no waste motion. (line 20)
4. A woman's wider pelvis, designed for *childbearing*, . . . (line 21)
5. . . . she displays a bit of a *jiggle and sway* as she walks. (line 23)
6. The angle at which a woman's *thigh* is joined to her knees . . . (line 27)
7. . . . makes climbing *awkward* for her, . . . (line 27)
8. . . . men *wrinkle* less than women do. (line 32)
9. The fat layer helps *insulate* them against heat. (line 38)

COLUMN B

a) having babies
b) have lines in their skin
c) silly
d) frightening
e) difficult
f) get tired
g) movement from side to side
h) understanding children
i) top part of leg
j) place in body where air goes when you breathe in
k) hide
l) put a leg forward to walk
m) protect
n) cold

JANE EHRENFELD

Inference

Sometimes you can find information in a text that is not stated clearly by the words there. You infer the information – that is, you make a logical guess – either from what is in the text, or by using your knowledge of the world, or both.

Try to infer the probable answers to these questions by looking at the text; be ready to give your reasons.

1. What happens during surgery that makes it riskier for men?
2. Name one part of the body where lead goes when it is breathed in.
3. Whose knees are more likely to be hurt by the same activities, men's or women's?
4. Name one advantage a man would have and one advantage a woman would have in a hot, sunny country.
5. If a man and woman weighed the same at age 20, who would be the stronger at age 60?

22 Getting to the airport

Here is a column from a newspaper about people's attitudes toward catching planes. Read it carefully, stopping when you want. Feel free to read it more than once.

AFTER YEARS OF STUDY, I have determined there are only two types of people in this world: those who get to the airport early and those who stroll in as
5 the plane is about to take off.

If there were any justice in this world, the early-airport people would be rewarded for doing the right thing. And the late-airport people would be punished.
10 But there is no justice. The early-airport people get ulcers, heart attacks and bite their fingernails to the bone.

The late-airport people barely are aware they are flying.
15 I once found myself in an airport bar with a man on the same flight as me. Our flight had been called three times, but he insisted we stay for another round.

"If we miss this one, there's always an-
20 other plane in an hour," he said, signaling for two more drinks.

"TO DHAHRAN, SAUDI ARABIA?" I said. "There isn't another flight for a week."
25 "I have a theory," he said. "If you miss your flight, it's because God didn't want you to go."

This is clearly a guy who is never going to get an ulcer.
30 Early-airport people suffer another

abuse. They are called exactly what they are: wimps.

I know. I was an early-airport person for years.

MY LUGGAGE WILL GET on the plane 35
first, I told myself.

Indeed it will. Which makes it the last luggage they take off the plane when you land.

You know who really gets his luggage 40
first? The late-airport person, who saunters into the airport three minutes before the plane takes off.

The pilot is practically in the air when these people are still paying off the taxi. 45

Then they make a big fuss at the gate in order to get their luggage on board.

And when we finally take off, all us wimps know that not only will that late luggage be the first off the plane, but it 50
is probably sitting on top of our luggage, crushing our shirts.

BUT IF I GET THERE real, real early, I told my old wimpy self, I will get the best seat. 55

Well, just try to show up early and get the seat you want. Go ahead and try.

No matter how early I showed up, I was always told that someone had called two

60 or three years ahead of me and asked for that seat.

I figured it was a conspiracy. I figured there was someone in America who called every airline every day and said: "Is that
65 wimp Simon flying somewhere today? If he is, give me his seat."

THE ULTIMATE EMBARRASSMENT of the early-airport person happened to me a few years ago when I was flying
70 from La Guardia to O'Hare.

When I got to the ticket counter, the person there said: "Sir, you have a seat on the 9:15 a.m. flight to Chicago, is that right?"
75 "Yes," I said.

"Well, it's only 7 a.m., and the 7:05 a.m. flight has not left yet. If you hurry, you can make it."

I was too embarrassed to say that I arrived at airports early so I wouldn't 80 have to hurry. Instead, I ran down the corridor to the plane.

I climbed on board, out of breath, red-faced, and stumbled over a woman's legs to get to the last unoccupied seat. 85

The woman I stepped over was no wimp. She had the guts to complain. "You should get to the airport earlier!" she snapped at me.

"I was here early," I said weakly. "But 90 then somehow I wasn't anymore."

AFTER A LIFETIME OF arguing over whether I really have to pack 24 hours in advance and set the alarm clock four hours ahead, I have learned one other 95 fact about early-airport people and late-airport people:

They always marry each other.

ulcers: damage to the inside of the stomach, caused partly by worry
wimp: coward, person with no courage (informal)
La Guardia, O'Hare: airports in New York and Chicago

Summary skills

Look back at the text to complete the table.

	Early-airport person	Result	Late-airport person	Result
Worries?				
Luggage on plane?	first	last off plane	last	first off plane
Anxious about seat?				
Marriage partner?				

Guessing words from context

Find single words in the text that seem to correspond to the definitions given below.

Example (in lines 62–89): passage between two or more larger spaces
Answer: corridor

Now find words for these meanings in lines 1–21:
1. walk in a relaxed way
2. reward for goodness, punishment for evil
3. one drink for each of a group of people

Find words for these meanings in lines 62–89:
4. evil plan
5. almost fell
6. courage

Inference

Try to imagine what would happen in the following situations.

1. When would an early-airport person begin studying for a test that was three weeks away? And a late-airport person?
2. When do early-airport people pay their telephone bills? And late-airport people?
3. Name at least two things an early-airport person does (but a late-airport person doesn't do) before a long trip.
4. Is an early-airport person's luggage ever searched by customs officers? And a late-airport person's luggage?

23   How personality affects your health

Reading for specific information

On the next page you will find the beginning of a book about how
personality is linked to the risk of heart attacks. Before you read the whole
text, practice looking for specific information by answering these questions
as quickly as you can.

1. The book is based on a study. How long did the study last?
2. How many people took part in the study?
3. The book talks about a certain type of person. Name one thing that type
   of person has trouble finding the time to do.
4. Are the people the book talks about all men?
5. In the study, what category of women had the most heart disease of all?
6. Do the people the book talks about usually do well in school?
7. Do they usually express anger when they feel it?

Now read the text, more than once if you want. Feel free to think about
what you have read.

Here are six questions about your approach to life. Try to answer them as honestly as you can. You may find the results revealing.

- Are you hard driving and competitive?
- Are you usually pressed for time?
- Are you bossy or dominating?   5
- Do you have a strong need to excel in most things?
- Do you eat too quickly?
- Do you get upset when you have to wait for anything?

If you have answered "yes" to most of these questions then I can make a few predictions about you, based on a recent eight-year study of nearly two   10
thousand people who live the way that you do.

You probably find that life is full of challenges and you often need to keep two or more projects moving at the same time. The chances are that you have been to college, that you have a management job and that you bring work home at night. You think that you put more effort into your job than many of the   15
people you work with, and you certainly take your work more seriously than most of them. You get irritated easily, and if someone is being long-winded, you help them get to the point. You also have trouble finding the time to get your hair cut.

And there's one other thing. You are about twice as likely to have a heart   20
attack as someone who takes a more easygoing approach to life.

The mention of heart attacks probably makes you think that surveys like this only apply to men. After all, men up to middle age in the United States and Britain have about four times more coronaries than women do. But women suffer too, if they adopt this same hard-driving, competitive, time-urgent life-   25
style. Working women living this way are twice as likely to develop coronary disease as those who are more relaxed.

You might expect things to be different for housewives, since living at home should cause less hassle than going out to work, and as a group, housewives in this study were more easygoing. But some felt the same time pressures as   30
women with outside jobs; the sense that things would get out of control unless they tried all the time to keep on top. Those who felt this suffered three times as much heart disease as those who didn't, whether they looked after an office or a home. And women with children, who were married to blue-collar workers and were holding down clerical jobs at the same time, had the highest heart   35
disease risk of all.

The beginnings of your hard-driving behavior go right back to childhood. In school you got recognition and perhaps prizes for being quick and bright, for being an achiever, for competing with others and *for winning*. You probably went on from school to get a series of increasingly better jobs against pretty   40
stiff competition. They were jobs where you had to care about the results, where you constantly had to push things forward and get things done. In your present job you also feel some conflict, either with time or with other people. Some of those you work with don't seem able to grasp the simplest ideas, and they often put a brake on what you're trying to achieve. The conflict may not   45
erupt every day. You pride yourself on being able to keep the lid on. But it's always there, under the surface.

revealing: Revealing results show you something.   *being long-winded:* talking too much
hard driving: always trying hard to get things done   *blue-collar:* A blue-collar job needs physical strength.
challenges: difficult jobs to be done successfully   *clerical:* office
projects: pieces of work done over a period of time

Inference

The person described in the text, whose life-style is likely to lead to a heart attack, is called a "Type A" person. Can you guess which of the following would be true of "Type B" people, who are not likely to have heart attacks?

1. They move more slowly than Type A people.
2. They are almost always men.
3. At meetings, they sit back in their chairs in a relaxed way.
4. They are good listeners.
5. They sometimes wait a few seconds before answering a question.
6. They feel they must succeed in everything they do.
7. They don't hurry decisions, but take time to think things over.
8. They feel that the only way to get a job done well is to do it themselves.
9. They take time to enjoy their food.
10. It doesn't bother them much to wait in line.

Guessing words from context

Find words or expressions in the text that seem to correspond to the definitions given below.

Example: a word in lines 22–27 that means "heart attacks"
Answer: coronaries (line 24)

1. an expression in lines 3–8 that means "in a hurry"
2. an expression in lines 12–19 that means "it is likely"
3. a word in lines 28–36 that means "trouble"
4. an expression in lines 28–36 that means "stay in control"

Find words for these meanings in lines 37–47:
5. somebody who did well
6. difficult
7. understand

Making connections

Misunderstandings sometimes happen because we do not realize what is meant by a word like *she* or *it*. Practice making this connection by giving the meaning of each word or phrase in italics.

1. ... you help *them* get to the point. (line 18)
2. ... as *those* who are more relaxed. (line 27)
3. ... unless *they* tried all the time to keep on top. (line 32)
4. *Those* who felt *this* suffered ... (line 32)
5. ... and *they* often put a brake on ... (line 45)
6. But *it's* always there, ... (line 46)

24 Wonder wander

Read this poem as many times as you want before doing the exercises.

in the afternoon the children walk like ducks
like geese
like from here to there
eyeing bird-trees puppy dogs candy windows
sun balls ice cream wagons   5
lady bugs rose bushes fenced yards vacant lots
tall buildings
and other things
big business men take big business walks
wear big business clothes   10
carry big business briefcases   talk about
big business affairs in
big business voices
young girls walk pretty on the streets
stroll the avenues linger by   15
shop windows   wedding rings   lady hats
shiny dresses   fancy shoes
whisper like turkey hens   passing the time
young men stride on parade   dream headed
wild eyed   eating up the world   20
with deep glances   rubbing empty fingers
in the empty pockets and
planning
me, I wander around soft-shoed   easy-legged
watching the scene as it goes   25
finding things   sea-gull feathers   pink baby roses
everytime I see a letter on the sidewalk
I stop and look   it might be
for me

Summary skills

This poem has five parts. On which line does each part begin?

Guessing words from context

Use the text to guess the probable meaning of each word.

1. *briefcases* (line 11): They are probably made of ＿＿＿＿＿＿＿
   and probably contain ＿＿＿＿＿＿＿＿ .
2. *linger* (line 15): If young girls do it by shop windows to see wedding
   rings, lacy hats, etc., it probably means ＿＿＿＿＿＿ .
3. *turkey* (line 18): The word *hens* tells you that this is a kind of ＿＿＿＿.
4. *sea-gull* (line 26): *Feathers* tells you that this is probably a ＿＿＿＿＿.

Vocabulary links

Find as many words as you can that have to do with:

1. walking
2. talking
3. animals
4. clothing
5. seeing

Attitudes and feelings 1

1. Which group of people do you think the narrator ("me") has the least
   sympathy for?
2. Which group of people do you think the narrator has the most
   sympathy for?

Attitudes and feelings 2

Here is a list of descriptions. Choose the most appropriate description for
each person or group of people in the poem. There are some extra
descriptions.

a) Wishing dreamily
b) Looking and hoping
c) Disappointed
d) Worried
e) Open to everything
f) Ambitious
g) Slowly becoming angry
h) Busy

Credits

The author and publisher are grateful to the following for permission to reproduce reading texts and illustrations. Page 2: "How to Shine at a Job Interview" by Richard K. Irish reprinted by permission of Sterling Lord Agency, Inc., © 1978 by Richard K. Irish. Page 6: Excerpts from "How to Protect Yourself" by Officer Gayle Orr reprinted from the May 10 issue of *Family Circle Magazine*, © 1983 The Family Circle, Inc. Page 10: Excerpt on how to carry out resuscitation from *How to Hold a Crocodile* by the Diagram Group, © 1981 by Diagram Visual Information Limited. Page 14: Excerpts from "How to Win at Marriage" © 1983 by Susan Starr Richards and first published in the March 1983 issue of *Ms*; photograph of Henry Fonda and Olivia de Havilland in *The Male Animal* courtesy of Culver Pictures, Inc. Page 16: Cartoon by Artemas Cole appeared in *New Woman* Magazine, December 1983, and is reprinted with permission of Artemas Cole and *New Woman* Magazine, © 1983 by *New Woman* Magazine. Page 18: "Athens Is Dying" was originally published under the title "A City Is Dying." © 1979 by Time Inc. All rights reserved. Reprinted by permission from *Time*. Photograph by Michael Freeman © 1978 by Time-Life Books B.V. from The Great Cities series. Page 20: Cartoon by Harpur © Punch/Rothco. Page 22: Excerpt from *Zen and the Art of Motorcycle Maintenance* by Robert M. Pirsig © 1974 by Robert M. Pirsig, reprinted by permission of William Morrow & Co. and the Bodley Head Ltd. Page 26: Excerpt on Mexico reprinted from *Mexico – Fun in the Sun*, a brochure published by the Secretaria de Turismo and the Consejo Nacional de Turismo. Page 28: Center photograph courtesy of Hyatt International Corporations and Hyatt Hotels Mexico; remaining photographs courtesy of the Mexico Ministry of Tourism. Page 30: Excerpt from *The Pine Barrens* by John McPhee © 1967, 1968 by John McPhee. Reprinted by permission of Farrar, Straus & Giroux, Inc. This material first appeared in *The New Yorker*. Page 34: Article originally appeared as "What Are the Effects of Power on People?" by Dr. Joyce Brothers, reprinted by permission of King Features Syndicate, Inc., © 1983 by King Features Syndicate, Inc. Page 36: "Smoke Signals" by David Holmstrom reprinted by permission of *American Way*, inflight magazine of American Airlines. Copyright 1983 by American Airlines. Page 40: Photograph courtesy of the South African Tourism Board. Page 41: Article consists of excerpts from "Family Life of Lions," by Des and Jen Bartlett, *National Geographic*, December 1982. Page 42: Photograph by Moira and Rod Borland/Bruce Coleman Inc. – New York. Page 44: Cartoon by Bil Keane reprinted courtesy of Cowles Syndicate, Inc. All rights reserved. "Burnout" excerpted with permission of *USA Today*. Page 48: "The Diamond" is an excerpt from the story "Out of the Fountain" in *The Story of a Non-Marrying Man* by Doris Lessing. Copyright 1972 Doris Lessing. Reprinted by permission of Jonathan Clowes Ltd., London, on behalf of the Doris Lessing Trust. Page 52: "A Gentleman Thief" first printed as "Nor Iron Bars," © 1980 by Time Inc. All rights reserved. Reprinted by permission from *Time*. Page 56: Cartoon by Michael Ffolkes by courtesy of Michael Ffolkes. Pages 56–7: Excerpts from *Great Operatic Disasters* by Hugh Vicker reprinted with permission of St. Martin's Press, Inc., New York; and Macmillan, London and Basingstoke, London. Copyright 1979 by Hugh Vickers. Page 60: Article on dioxin originally appeared as "Dioxin Problems in Times Beach Began in 1971" and is used by permission of The Associated Press. Page 62: Photograph by Scott Dine, courtesy of Scott Dine. Page 65: Advertisement of the family room courtesy of Ethan Allen, Inc. Page 66: "Some Things Are Better Left Unsaid" originally appeared in *Woman's Day Magazine*, © 1982 by Eda LeShan. Page 68: Save the Children advertisement courtesy of Save the Children Federation, Inc. Page 72: Article is an excerpt from *What Every Woman Should Know about Men* by Dr. Joyce Brothers, reprinted by permission of Simon & Schuster, Inc. Copyright 1982 by Joyce B. Enterprises, Inc. Page 74: Illustration courtesy of Jane Ehrenfeld. Page 76: Article originally appeared as "Tardiness Is a Virtue at Airports," by Roger Simon, © 1983 Los Angeles Times Syndicate, reprinted with permission. Page 79: Illustration by Jean-François Allaux, courtesy of Jean-François Allaux. Page 80: Text is excerpted from *Slipping into Overdrive* by Clive Wood, reprinted by permission of Fontana Paperbacks and A. D. Peters & Co. Ltd. Page 82: "Wonder Wander" by Leonore Kandel reprinted from *I Took My Mind a Walk*, edited by George Sanders and published by Penguin Books Ltd., London.

Illustrations on pages 3, 7, 33, 37, 66, 76 by Mary Jo Quay
Illustrations on pages 12, 46, 57, 58, 61 by Gene Reynolds

Map on page 27 by Glen Burris
Illustration on page 48 by Judith Gwyn Brown

Book design by Peter Ducker
Cover design by Frederick Charles Ltd.
Cover photograph by Mary Jo Quay